"*SNAP Yes! The Art of Seeing New Achievable Possibilities in Business and Life* is a well-written, insightful, and most of all motivating book. It does not matter what you are facing in life—whether you are feeling 'stuck' in a relationship or your business is struggling—the bottom-line message is to take responsibility and move into action. In a day and age where it seems people want to 'blame' parents, the economy, or the government, DeDe's book helps motivate people to change what they are able to change and to take action. Take a step out of the box you have created for yourself, and take a risk on what gives you passion, purpose, and meaning!"
—Earl Henslin, PsyD, BCETS, Psychotherapist, Author, "Brain
    Doctor"

"All action begins in the mind. If you're to change your world, you must first change your thinking. I've always lived by this truth and shared it with my audiences, clients, and students—and clearly, DeDe Murcer Moffett agrees. Her book simply and brilliantly conveys that we live constricted lives only because we believe we must. Change that belief, and life opens up in amazing ways. It's a message America really needs to hear right now."
—Nido Qubein, Speaker, Author, Consultant, Founder of National
    Speakers Association Foundation, President of High Point University

"To me, DeDe ranks way up there as a writer and a lecturer with the Wayne Dyers or the Zig Ziglars of today. I am ordering five copies for our adult children as soon as it becomes available."
—Fritz Peterson, Former New York Yankees Pitcher, Author of *When
    the Yankees Were On the Fritz: Revisiting the "Horace Clarke Era"*

"*SNAP Yes!* is an incredible extension of DeDe's unsurpassed energy in print. James Bryce wrote, 'The worth of a book is to be measured by what you can carry away from it.' Bryce was not a prophet seeing the future but he could well have been envisioning *SNAP Yes!* If this book fails to jolt even the most resistant among us, leading us into the action required to truly fully empower our own lives, then lightning isn't electric!"

—Eldon Taylor, PhD, FAPA, *New York Times* Best-selling Author
   of *Choices and Illusions*

"Wow! What a triumph of transformation, positivity, and courage! Since I love sports and have worked with many professional teams, I was first drawn to DeDe's stories about her uncle, the great baseball player Bobby Murcer. But what really grabbed me was her honesty, her raw energy, and her conviction that life can be so much more than most people settle for. Don't just say *yes* to this book. Say SNAP Yes!"

—Jon Gordon, Keynote Speaker, Best-selling Author of *The Energy
   Bus: 10 Rules to Fuel Your Life, Work, and Team with Positive
   Energy* and *Training Camp: What the Best Do Better Than
   Everyone Else*

"Many conferences today forget that attendees need more than just educational sessions. They need motivation, inspiration, and authentic leaders who can excite not only the mind but more importantly ignite the heart. That's the power of DeDe Murcer Moffett. You walk away from her talks with the conviction and the tools to See New Achievable Possibilities that will allow you to step into your spotlight of success."

—Esther Spina, Speaker, Entrepreneur, Author of *The Ambitious
   Woman: What It Takes and Why You Want to Be One*

"DeDe's book *SNAP Yes!* is written from the heart of her own transformational life experience. It is filled with inspiration and hope for anyone who has lost their sense of joy and purpose in life—whatever their dreams may be. It is filled with practical advice and motivating stories of others who have 'SNAP-ed to life.' In a time when so many have deadened themselves with addictions, distractions, and empty doing, DeDe will guide you back to finding meaning and joy in your life."
—Joseph Bailey, Psychologist, Author of *Slowing Down to the Speed of Life, The Serenity Principle,* and many other books

"DeDe keeps everyone wanting more! The information is relevant to business, life, and athletics. Thoroughly enjoyed every minute!"
—Gary Trost, First Vice President, United States Professional Tennis Association

"DeDe Murcer Moffett is brilliant! She is absolutely the most intelligent, energetic, and entertaining individual! In her book *SNAP Yes!* DeDe is open and brutally honest about her own life, to which many will be able to relate. DeDe teaches, captivates, and inspires on both a personal and business level. Once you start reading this book, you will not want to put it down."
—Dr. Jeretta Horn Nord, Professor, Entrepreneur, Author of *A Cup of Cappuccino for the Entrepreneur's Spirit* Series

SNAP
Yes!

The Art of
Seeing **N**ew **A**chievable **P**ossibilities
in Business and Life

DeDe Murcer Moffett

Published by:
Out of the Box Publishing
P.O. Box 5595
Frisco, TX 75035
www.dedemurcermoffett.com

ISBN: 978-0-9974373-0-0

Library of Congress Control Number: 2016905004

Printed in the United States of America

To all those who feel the pull of their dreams—and are willing
to find their spotlight and stand in it!

Contents

How I Finally Said SNAP Yes!

This is a book about the boxes we find ourselves trapped in. It's about how the boxes got built in the first place, why we choose to stay in them, and what we do to make our situations bearable. And it's about what happens when we SNAP!—when we kick down those walls that prevent us from Seeing New Achievable Possibilities in our lives.

The box I speak of is a mindset—an extremely powerful and debilitating one that limits our perspective and prevents us from living our best life. For many years I was trapped in one of the darkest, loneliest, most soul-robbing boxes of all. And as grateful as I am to have broken free, I'm also grateful for the box itself. Those painful years played a big role in making me who I am today.

Like all boxes, construction on mine began in childhood. Both of my parents were very young and neither of *them* had parents who were ideal role models. Frankly, they were both trying to survive the limiting messages they adopted from their parents and they were divorced by the time I was eight—so along the way, I'm sure I internalized some messages they never meant to send.

Now let me say upfront that I DO NOT blame my parents for my life choices. There's no doubt in my mind that they loved me and wanted the best for me. But like all well-meaning parents, they wanted to protect me. All those *Don't do this*-es and *Don't do that*-s meant to keep me safe got internalized as, *The world is not a safe place, so don't take too many risks.*

The messages we "hear" in childhood (however unintended and mostly inaccurate) end up influencing our life choices to a scary degree, without our even being conscious we can choose differently. We don't even realize it's happening. In my particular case, I came to believe that I wasn't "strong enough" or "smart enough" to figure life out on my own. I needed someone else to tell me what and how to do…me.

This belief manifested first in my dating life. In high school I got involved with a guy who was a popular athlete. At the time I actually felt honored he was interested in me. But soon, the abuse began. This guy was insanely jealous. He hit me, tried to drown me, held a knife to my throat, cut off my hair, slashed all four of my tires, and even threatened boys who were just my friends. It got really crazy when he began to call my house and tell my mother, "I'm going to kill your daughter."

We dated on and off for five years. I just kept trying to figure out what I was doing wrong. Why didn't he love me enough to not beat me up? What I should have been asking was why I didn't love myself enough to end the relationship. The need to make someone love me—all the while feeling distinctly *un*lovable—was part of the box I was building for myself. I had a "man hole" in my soul and I let it completely distract me from pursuing my hopes and dreams.

I've since learned that when you are emotionally unhealthy, you're drawn to unhealthy partners. And if you find a healthy partner—one who won't "do your dance" of dysfunction—you'll sabotage the relationship. This was a pattern that was to play out over and over in my life. It's why my marriage to my first husband—an incredibly nice guy from Australia—fell apart.

The box I was trapped in also kept me from my dream career. Ever since childhood, I had been singing and dancing and dreaming of someday going to Broadway. Yet when I got the chance of a lifetime to study vocal performance at the same college that Kristin Chenoweth attended...I blew it!

Driven by insecurity and fear, I traded my Broadway dreams for a life that felt safe. It was very important to me to be financially self-sufficient—to not be "a burden" in life—so I looked around for a career that would let me make lots of money. I started working in sales and soon I got pretty successful.

Oh, and I was successful in a man's world. I sold Toyota forklifts in Oklahoma, Northern California, and Texas. I was one of the first females to get in the industry and become successful despite the attitude that a woman couldn't compete in the good old boys' club. (This was a big "fork you" moment!)

I also sold trash—well, trash *removal*—as well as collateral protection insurance and other insurance products to banks and credit unions. I even sold people! I spent some time as a sales recruiter putting the right people with the right companies. So do I know what motivates and de-motivates salespeople? SNAP Yes! And it ain't always the money.

I made lots of money, but the work didn't make me happy. Just because you're good at something doesn't mean you should do it for the rest of your life! Oh, no one would ever have known. My survival strategy, which I had honed in childhood, was to act as if nothing bothered me. I became a high-energy, outspoken, "happy" person. ("Hey, I like living in this box. Don't you love how I've decorated it?") And I had another survival strategy as well: alcohol.

It turned out that I REALLY liked alcohol. It quieted the voices in my head and made all my anxiety melt away. And so I soon developed a little (okay, maybe not so little) drinking problem—and I remained an alcoholic for the next 24 years.

Oh, I was a very high-functioning drunk. Early in my drinking career, I worked full time and taught three aerobics classes each day—one in the morning, one at lunch, and one at night. I could drink until I passed out and still get up early, completely hung over, and teach my 5:30 a.m. aerobics class—kicking everyone's butt. My thinking was, *If I can do that, then I can't be an alcoholic!*

And as my sales career progressed, I found that drinking helped me cope with my deep unhappiness and my Broadway regrets. I was making a good living, building relationships with customers, and even winning awards, but what I really wanted to do was entertain people, make them think, and touch them in deep, life-changing ways. I didn't hate my job in Corporate America but it also didn't make me come alive. And so I drank to "numb out" my life. That's the definition of crazy. If you have to numb out your life to do your life, then maybe you should take a second or third look at your life…and SNAP the hell out of it!

Because I looked so "together" on the surface, no one realized I had a serious addiction. I had the right look, the right house, the right car. I laughed a lot. I had plenty of friends. I kept racking up sales at work. So no one called me on my drinking. And I refused to sit still long enough to take a good look at my life. I was too busy overcompensating and desperately trying to convince myself (and everyone else) that everything was okay.

Right after my first marriage ended, my father died of lung cancer at the age of 47. I was 26 and that's when life really started to spin out of control. I bought a Harley motorcycle, rode from bar to bar to bar with my friends, married my second husband (who turned out to be an abusive jerk), moved to California, had a "close call" suicide attempt and a stint in rehab that ultimately failed, got a divorce, moved to Dallas, and continued to spin faster and faster for another 10 years. It may seem odd to gloss right over such devastating life events, but that's how it felt to me: like it all flew by in a blur, barely touching me. I look back on this time as my "Tasmanian devil" years.

Once in Dallas, I attempted the theatre thing again. I fell right back into it like I'd never been away. I was instantly selected for lead roles and did three amazing shows, but somehow this success made me even sadder. Regret would kick in and I'd think, *With a little more effort, what could I have done? Where would I be today?* So ultimately, I just shut down, stopped auditioning, even quit listening to Streisand and Garland. The whole thing just made me want to drink even more.

Then I got really caught up in corporate projects. Now I realize this was justification for not living the life that really lit me up. I thought making and spending money would take the longing away, but dreams don't die—they just keep tapping you on the shoulder, hoping you will wake the hell up!

Then, I met a man who would change my life forever. I was at a conference in Florida and we met at a bar—go figure, huh?—and stayed up all night drinking and talking. Soon we met at another conference (we ran in the same industry circles) and started a relationship.

Here was a man who was as successful as me and who had his life together. I was very attracted to that. And we had so much fun at the beginning: travel, nice dinners, bottles of wine. Oh, the wine! About a year into the relationship, *he* would have two glasses and *I* would have two bottles. It started to be a problem. It got to where before we had a big client dinner Rick would warn me, "Okay, DeDe, don't drink all the wine."

Anyway, we had gotten engaged. Then, on a Friday the 13th just two months away from the wedding, we were at a conference in Austin. I had 13 glasses of wine. (Hmm, I just noticed a pattern!) Rick did just about everything he could to distract me from my drinking. Of course my response was, "I don't have a problem! Would you look at me, I am a professional!" So, as you can imagine, the tension between us was like a rubber band stretched to its limits. But I kept telling myself there would always be more give in that rubber band.

I was wrong. The morning after my 13-glasses-of-wine, act-like-a-fool, pass-out-on-the-table drunk-fest, everything had changed. Rick had snapped and he was done.

He made it clear that the engagement was over, the wedding was off, and he wasn't living the rest of his life in a box with a full-blown alcoholic. Good for him, right? It was (although it didn't feel good at the time). But it was the best thing that ever happened to me. That's because when he snapped, I FINALLY WOKE UP, STOOD UP (albeit slowly), and SNAP-ed OUT OF IT.

I knew he was serious and I knew that I absolutely *could not* lose this man. I truly loved him. And so I begged. I pleaded. I promised I would never drink again. Of course, he didn't believe me at first. (I didn't believe me, either!) Who would, with my track record?

That was back in 2007, and I have kept my promise to Rick and to myself. It has not always been easy, and it took a few years for our relationship to stabilize. But as tough as it has been to get sober and to rebuild the way I see and do every single thing in life, each step has been absolutely worth it.

Have I wanted to drink? Hell yes. But I made the choice not to. I don't like the words "I can't drink" because that makes me sound and feel like a victim with no control. But when I tell the truth, when I say, "Yes, I want to drink but I choose not to," that puts everything in the right perspective. I have the power; I'm not powerless. I have a choice; I'm not a victim. I have the ability to change my life in a SNAP!

So yes, when Rick snapped, I SNAP-ed. I was able for the first time in my life to break out of the box I had built for myself. I could finally <u>S</u>ee <u>N</u>ew <u>A</u>chievable <u>P</u>ossibilities for myself. I realized I had to learn to live in a whole different way and that I had to start feeling my life before I could change it. That meant confronting my regrets about what "might have been" and training my focus on what still might be.

And so—in the midst of a lot of soul searching, fear facing, excuse kicking, and choice making—I found my "big balls of courage." I set out to create a new career as a speaker and entertainer with a message. I feel that today my calling is to inspire, motivate, and move people to act. Not because I think they should but because I now know it is possible to find your spotlight and confidently stand in it. I know it's possible to do what you think you can't, and it's absolutely possible to <u>S</u>ee <u>N</u>ew <u>A</u>chievable <u>P</u>ossibilities in every area of your life.

It won't surprise you to learn that these days I incorporate theatre and entertainment into my speaking. I sing, I dance, and I act.

Fairly soon my one-woman show will hit the stage. It's an autobiography about my struggle with alcoholism, but more than that, it's about our collective struggle with addictions, distractions, and whatever will take us out of the present moment. This is something I will do—something I MUST do—before I exit this place.

I have lived out some big dreams since I SNAP-ed out of it, like singing the national anthem for my favorite team in the world, the New York Yankees, at Yankee Stadium; for the NBA's Oklahoma City Thunder; and for many other professional organizations…but I'm just getting started!

Has all of this been hard and exhausting? SNAP Yes! Am I glad I broke out of the box? *DOUBLE* SNAP Yes! It turns out that feeling my life fully is what living fully lit is all about. This has led to a rich, full, challenging, messy, joyful life that I no longer wish to numb out—a life I feel honored and proud to live.

Still, staying sober and emotionally healthy—staying *conscious*—is a lifelong journey and struggle. But I feel a huge sense of responsibility to those who watch my life and hear me speak. People continuously share with me their stories of how drug and alcohol abuse has damaged their lives. It might be their addiction or it might be the addiction of someone in their family or circle of influence. These stories, however painful to me, have become my touchstones. They remind me of where I have been and why I chose to go where I am going. These people and the audiences who hear me speak are each and collectively my accountability partners, and I am so incredibly grateful for them.

And I am grateful to *you*, my readers, for caring enough to spend time with me throughout this book. Yes, I broke out of my box (at least, many of them). I am still busting through boxes as I create my life. You can do the same, no matter how hopeless, numb, bored, or dreary you may feel right now. You just have to SNAP!

Stop just going through the motions and fully immerse yourself in what you're doing—at work, in your relationships, and in the experiences that add color and texture to your life. Once you do that, everything changes. Authentic engagement opens doors you never realized were there. And life won't just change for you but also for your team—your family, your friends, and your tribe—everyone who walks the path with you.

It's time to say SNAP Yes! to living, loving, and leading a SNAP-tastic life. But get ready 'cause it's a helluva ride! Can I get a SNAP Yes? Can I get a SNAP Yes?!?

The High Price of Living a Boxed-in Life

Our country is in the middle of an epidemic that's dulling America's spirit, squelching our potential, and sapping our happiness. I'm NOT talking about some infectious disease, or the obesity crisis, or even our obsession with the Kardashians (though God knows that's not helping). I'm talking about a viral wave of *disengagement*. As a culture we're tuned out, turned off, and frankly just going through the motions.

This is true in every area of life, but since we spend so much time at work—and since work funds all the rest of it—let's start there. People, too many of us are just phoning it in. (Is that still a thing? Or now do we say texting it in?)

When I speak to companies and professional groups, I hear about disengagement all the time. C-suiters, supervisors, and front-line employees all describe a concerning lack of motivation, energy, and commitment in the workplace. This is not anecdotal handwringing: The numbers back it up. According to a recent Gallup poll,[1] less than 30 percent of American workers are engaged in their jobs. In other words, over two-thirds of us spend a good chunk of our waking hours feeling unenthusiastic, unmotivated, and unfulfilled.

Common sense tells us that employee disengagement hurts the economy, and sure enough it does—to the tune of $450 to $550 *billion*[2] in lost productivity per year. It hurts society too. Think about it: How many scientific breakthroughs, time-saving innovations, and life-improving products never come into existence because the people who could have created them were counting down the minutes until 5:00? (It's the "George Bailey" effect applied to the workplace.)

But if the bankers and CEOs will pardon me for saying so, the economic cost of disengagement isn't even the worst part. The real tragedy is the negative impact it has on us as individuals.

When we aren't engaged in our jobs, we probably aren't engaged in our lives outside of work either. You don't flip a switch at quitting time and suddenly become a vibrant, creative, self-actualized person. It just doesn't work that way. Engagement is a *way of being*—which means disengagement at work is just a symptom of disengagement in life.

When we're disengaged, we aren't really *living*. We don't move forward with passion and purpose; we drift aimlessly from one day to the next. We can't grow, connect, and contribute when we're distracted, numbed out, and feeling powerless and hopeless.

Why do we settle for such a dismal existence? Surely we didn't choose this life—did we? Well, yes. It might be convenient to blame your boss, the economy, Congress, or Fate. But these are just scapegoats. When you're disengaged in life, it's probably because you are boxed in by self-limiting beliefs. That's right. You are living in a box of your own making. And since you built it, you can also tear it down.

Boxes Skew Your View—and Screw You Over!

If you read my story at the beginning of the book, you'll remember that I talked about living life in a box. By "box," I simply mean a powerful, draining mindset that limits your perspective and prevents you from living your best life.

When you live in a box, you tend to see limits, not possibilities. The world looks like a place of scarcity, not abundance. You believe that this is as good as it gets, that you can't do better for yourself, that you already have enough challenges on your plate, and that the life you *really* want is out of reach. And so you might as well hunker down, do what you have to do to get by, and pretty much just ride out the clock.

I'm speaking from experience here—remember, I spent decades living a life that literally drove me to drink (and trust me, being drunk is the pinnacle of disengagement) because I had convinced myself that I wasn't good enough to realize my true dream of being on Broadway.

That's a Well-Built Box. Have You Had It Your Whole Life?

Where do our boxes come from? We aren't born with them…but nevertheless, I believe their foundations are laid very early in life.

If you've been around children for more than five minutes, you know that they're naturally curious, vivacious, and vibrant. Any parent is sure to tell you something like, *Yes, I absolutely love these things about my kiddos—but in the hectic shuffle of everyday life, I don't always have the time or energy or stamina to let my children be themselves.* And so, most (if not all) of us end up hearing phrases like these during our growing-up years:

- *Be quiet.*
- *Be careful.*
- *Don't try to do that by yourself.*
- *Haven't I told you that already?*
- *Math isn't your best subject.*
- *Watch out, people will rip you off if you let them.*
- *Life's not fair.*
- *Don't mess with things you don't understand.*
- *Let me do that for you.*
- *Are you sure you want to do that?*
- *Don't do that—you'll get hurt.*
- *You're smarter than that.*

Let's look at that last phrase. When a child hears those words over and over again, the underlying message he receives is, *I must NOT be smarter than that—because I keep doing it!* This kid might spend his whole life playing it safe and settling for small victories because he believes he isn't smart enough to achieve anything great.

Similarly, phrases like *Stop doing that—you'll hurt yourself* send the message that taking risks is dangerous and evokes disapproval from important people. Yet when we become adults, we're told that within reason, risk-taking is admirable. How confusing!

I'm certain our parents, teachers, coaches, and other authority figures didn't mean to stifle us, suggest that we don't have what it takes to handle life's challenges, or saddle us with limiting beliefs. They were concerned with our well-being and were trying to keep us safe in the best way they knew how. (And, of course, they were working within their own self-limiting worldviews!)

Now that we're adults, it's up to us to take a close look at our foundational beliefs and where they might have originated—so that we can discard and replace those that are holding us back.

As I've said, a boxed-in mindset manifests itself throughout the 40 (or 50, or 60) hours a week you spend working. You don't try for the promotion you really want because you're convinced you're not qualified enough. You don't share the bold new marketing idea you had because you're sure the rest of the team will laugh it down. You don't apply for a transfer to the sales department because you're afraid the answer will be "no" (even though you believe you'd be really successful on the road).

And of course if you don't think you deserve great things at work (say, a raise or promotion), you'll settle for a mediocre personal existence, too—whether that's living in a stifling small town when you'd actually prefer a big, exciting city or spending your weekends lazing in front of the TV instead of joining an outdoors group or taking fun road trips.

If you don't think you have the guts (and maybe even the right) to speak up to a demanding, demeaning client, you might also choose to stay trapped in a bad marriage or to knuckle under every time your mother-in-law starts nagging.

If your social behavior at work is dictated by what you do (and don't) want your coworkers to think of you, so is your social behavior off the clock. (In which case, your friendships aren't authentic—and they may be downright toxic.) Boxes can make you choose to look a certain way, act a certain way, and even speak a certain way depending on whom you're trying to please.

Do you see what's happening here? At work, at home, in your relationships—in every aspect of your life!—you never give yourself a chance to succeed because you're already sure you'll fail. The crappy things you believe about yourself (which, by the way, probably aren't true) keep you trapped in a little-bitty box where you don't grow, thrive, or experience true joy and fulfillment. And guess what? *A whole lot* of us are living little-bitty (with apologies to Alan Jackson).

Eventually, Your Box Will Break You.

The smaller, more limiting your box is, the more it's costing you. Our boxes keep us from feeling excitement, confidence, and enthusiasm. They stop us from taking risks and getting to know ourselves. They hold us back from connecting to our passions and heeding our inner wisdom. They keep us feeling overwhelmed, overworked, and overdone. And sooner or later, our boxes make us so miserable that they prompt us to look for a way to numb out.

For me (and for everyone else who falls into the 30 percent[3] of Americans who have suffered from an alcohol-use disorder), booze was the answer. When I was drunk, I didn't have to think about how dissatisfied I was with my career, my relationships, and where my life was going. Other people turn to different substances—like illegal drugs and prescription medications—to achieve the same effect.

Even if you're a teetotaler who never pops a pill stronger than aspirin, don't feel smug! Shopping, gambling, eating, exercising, and vegging out on the couch for a four-hour Netflix marathon are all ways to keep yourself from feeling the claustrophobic effects of your box. For type-A, high-achiever personalities, staying perpetually busy and striving to be the "best" at everything can be a way to keep negative feelings at bay.

No matter what your numb-out method of choice is, the end result is the same: Your spirit breaks. You give up. You decide that it's never going to get any better, that high-flying dreams are for other people. You'd like to resign not just from your job but from your life…only, who would pay the bills and keep the house from falling apart?

It's Time to SNAP!

The GREAT news is that you can change your life at any time. Read that sentence again. What a powerful thought! And it's absolutely true. Just because you've meekly and complacently stayed in your box every day of your life up until now doesn't mean you have to stay in it for one more minute. You can SNAP right now. IT'S YOUR CHOICE. And ONLY you can make it.

Your box is never going to fall apart on its own. No one is going to dismantle it for you. And the longer you live with your self-limiting beliefs, the stronger that damn box will become. There's only one solution. If you want to discover what's outside the box, you'll have to bust out of it…and then drop-kick it as far away as you possibly can. (This will be one of the scariest, hardest, most liberating, and most joyful things you've ever done!)

That's where this book comes in. My goal is to get you to SNAP— or to See New Achievable Possibilities beyond the walls of your little-bitty box. What's more, I want to help you discover your power so that you can make those possibilities a reality. I promise, you have what it takes to get out of your box. When you SNAP, you will become happier, healthier, wealthier, and—yes—wiser, too. (Take it from this recovering alcoholic who has finally found her spotlight.)

Are you ready to get started? Are you ready to start believing that you deserve great things? Are you ready to discover the freedom that comes only with giving yourself permission to be who you truly are? If you're ready to SNAP into the exhilarating life you were always meant to live, then turn the page. So—can I get a SNAP Yes?!?

Endnotes

1 Adkins, Amy. "Majority of U.S. Employees Not Engaged Despite Gains in 2014." *Gallup*, January 28, 2015. Accessed February 22, 2016. http://www.gallup.com/poll/181289/majority-employees-not-engaged-despite-gains-2014.aspx.

2 Sorenson, Susan, and Keri Garman. "How to Tackle U.S. Employees' Stagnating Engagement." *Gallup*, June 11, 2013. Accessed February 22, 2016. http://www.gallup.com/businessjournal/162953/tackle-employees-stagnating-engagement.aspx.

3 Main, Douglas. "30 Percent of Americans Have Had an Alcohol-Use Disorder." *Newsweek*, June 3, 2015. Accessed 22 February, 2016. http://www.newsweek.com/30-percent-americans-have-had-alcohol-use-disorder-339085.

"It's unbelievable how much you don't know about the game you have been playing all your life."
—Mickey Mantle

Chapter 1

How Boxed in Are You?

If you're reading this, I assume you've made the decision to say SNAP Yes!, bust out of your box, and drop-kick it across the room. (Or at least you're thinking about sticking one toe out and cautiously testing the waters.) So...where to start? And how to find the energy? When you're boxed in, burned out, and buried in beliefs that are sucking the life out of you, the way forward can seem pretty darn murky. That's where this book comes in. Together, we'll break SNAP-ing up into baby steps.

Like a contractor who needs to demolish a building, you don't start by hauling out the wrecking ball. First, you need to assess the structure you're tearing down. How big is it? How strong is it? What's it made of? Are there any weak points? Places that might be super-dangerous or difficult to deconstruct? Basically, you need to figure out: *How boxed in am I?*

Fact is, many of us aren't just boxed in; we're wrapped in bubble wrap and then double-boxed, with a bunch of packing tape wrapped around for good measure. This chapter will help you to honestly assess the box you're living in so that you'll be well equipped to wield that wrecking ball when the time comes. (So keep your hard hat nearby!)

The Word That's Keeping You Stuck (and Making Your Life Suck)

There are a lot of indicators that you're even more securely packaged than the famous leg lamp from *A Christmas Story*. We'll talk about many of them in the next few pages, but first I want to highlight the biggest, brightest neon sign pointing to a boxed-in life: the word *no*.

Sure, *no* is a short, innocent-seeming word. It's two letters: How bad could it be? But those two letters pack quite a punch. In my experience, the more you say and think no, the more boxed in you are. How often do you respond to life's challenges, possibilities, and invitations with, *No, I can't do that.* Or, *No, that's not possible.* Or my personal favorite, *Hell no! That is* NOT *gonna happen!* If you're saying no more than you're saying yes, you are forcing yourself to live within self-imposed limits. You're repressing your interests and passions. You are settling for mediocre instead of magnificent.

If it isn't benefitting us, why is *no* such a big part of our vocabulary? Most of the time, our *noes* are driven by fear: Fear of failure. Fear of looking stupid. Fear of being uncomfortable. Fear of demolishing the status quo and stepping into the unknown. You get the picture.

For instance, when you say, "No, I don't think I'll accept the invitation to speak on a panel at the upcoming conference," you're really saying, "I'm afraid I'll look foolish in front of my peers, and that no one will respect the insights I have to share." In my case, "No, I don't think I'll move to New York and take my chances on Broadway," was simply another way of saying, "I'm afraid I'll never be cast in a performance, and that I'll become a penniless, prospect-less loser."

The problem is, over the course of a lifetime, fear-driven *noes* can steer you into a boxed-in life that's uninspiring and unfulfilling on every level. So, I have an assignment for you. Over the next 24 hours, pay attention to how often you say no. Ask yourself what you're afraid of. Then challenge yourself to imagine how your life could improve if you challenged your fear and responded with a big, loud, "SNAP Yes!"

Every Once in a While, Pop Culture Hits the Nail on the Head.

If you've never seen *Yes Man* starring Jim Carrey, make yourself a bowl of popcorn and watch it. The movie follows a pessimistic, cynical man who, at an inspirational seminar, promises to say *yes!* to every opportunity, invitation, and request he encounters over the next year. After ditching *no*, our hero's life is transformed. His friendships blossom, his career takes off, he picks up fulfilling hobbies—he even gets a girlfriend! Talk about SNAP-ing out of a box. Sure, *Yes Man* is a bit overblown and unrealistic in the way that Hollywood comedies usually are, but the point it makes is a solid one: What wonderful possibilities might be in store for you if you didn't reject them before they had a chance to develop?

If you're more of a reader than a film buff, you might want to check out Shonda Rhimes' new book, *Year of Yes: How to Dance It Out, Stand in the Sun, and Be Your Own Person.* (You might know Shonda from a few little shows she created, including *Grey's Anatomy* and *Scandal.*) In *Year of Yes,* Shonda writes about how she committed to saying yes to the invitations she received for one year, even when her introverted nature pushed her to say no. Spoiler alert: Saying yes pushed Shonda into the fear zone—and it also transformed her life in profoundly positive ways.

Now, despite all I've said so far, I do want to add that no isn't *always* a bad word. In some circumstances, it can be empowering. It can help you to draw healthy boundaries and keep your life from becoming cluttered with extraneous, uninspiring, and exhausting obligations: *No, I don't have time to take on that task. No, I'd rather not attend that event. No, I won't enable your destructive behavior.*

And if you look at this point from the flip side, you'll realize that *yes* can sometimes be harmful: *Yes, I'll join that committee...even though I'm really not drawn to its mission and don't have the extra time.*

In my experience, boxed-in people have real difficulty with using both *no* and *yes* in constructive ways. It's only after you've SNAP-ed that you'll start to feel more confident saying no to what does not enrich your life, and saying yes to what does—regardless of what others expect you to do.

Get to Know Your Box.

Now that we've covered the tyranny of *no*, I invite you to treat the rest of this chapter as an assessment to help you determine how boxed in you really are. It's not an exhaustive list, but if you answer each question honestly, you'll end up with a good working understanding of what your box looks like and how it's affecting your life.

What are your "life-saving" outlets? In my previous career, the one thing that kept me going all day was the thought of the drink (okay, many drinks) I'd have after I left the office. *Thank God for alcohol. It's such a lifesaver. I don't know what I'd do without it.* I also considered decorating my home and gardening to be essential lifesavers, albeit not as effective as drinking.

What about you? Which activities or habits do you cling to in order to make the rest of your daily existence bearable? Think eating, drinking, shopping, gambling, exercising, dating, etc. The number of lifesavers you have—and also how desperately you rely on them—indicates how boxed in and disengaged you really are. If you were living a purposeful, inspired life, you wouldn't feel the need to escape it.

Do you live by the "bare minimum" rule? Do you approach each task by wondering how little effort you can put forth and still get by? *How many corners can I cut without the boss reprimanding me? How can I demonstrate to my child's teacher that I'm a "caring, involved parent" without actually having to spend a bunch of time volunteering in the classroom?* Guess what? There's a good reason why you instinctively fight against spending your time and energy this way. You aren't allowing yourself to tap into your true talents and values.

Is it never your fault? How big is your arsenal of excuses? Do you blame other people and events for circumstances ranging from the city you live in to the work you do to why you can never seem to arrive to appointments on time? Rationalizing your life (and why it isn't the way you want it to be) protects you from discomfort and absolves you from the responsibility to take action, but it isn't a recipe for positive change. Excuses don't help you see *or* achieve new possibilities; they keep you trapped in your box. As I often say when I'm speaking: Excuses don't inspire. Excuses retire your options.

Are you driven by image? Many of us live in certain neighborhoods, drive certain cars, send our kids to certain schools, and spend our free time doing certain activities not because we *really* want to, but because we're concerned about how others will view us. We want to be seen as successful, put-together, cool, etc. We definitely *don't* want our families, friends, neighbors, and coworkers to think we're weird losers.

What's more, plenty of people stay in jobs they hate because they need the paycheck to maintain the type of lifestyle that they "deserve." (That was certainly true for me!) Others spend too much trying to maintain a successful, mainstream image—which leaves them perpetually broke and stressed out. What's happening here? We're putting our image before our happiness, and the lack of authenticity is killing us.

Do you feel alone? In our world of over 7 billion people, how many of your fellow humans do you feel connected to? Do you feel almost or totally alone? Do you believe that no one in your life really understands or cares about you? This is a common symptom of living a boxed-in life. When your limiting beliefs don't allow you to live an authentic, fulfilling life, it's no wonder that you have trouble forging authentic, fulfilling relationships. That sucks!

Have you lost that loving feeling? While thinking about your relationships, pay special attention to the one you have with your partner (if applicable). Are you with this person because he or she enriches your life, supports you, and encourages you to be the best possible version of yourself? Do you like *and* love your partner? Or are you settling? Maybe you feel that your boyfriend's or girlfriend's demeaning criticism is an acceptable price to pay for not being alone, or perhaps you're married only because you can't remember life without your spouse. While I would never advise taking or ending relationships lightly, I also know from personal experience that staying in a relationship solely out of habit, fear, or complacency is soul-crushing.

How strong is your self-esteem? For something that's emphasized so heavily in our younger years, a surprising number of adults are running *really* low on self-esteem. To gauge your levels, consider these questions: *Do I often say or think I'm not good enough or smart enough? Do I think mistakes and failures are bad, and a reflection on my worth as an individual? Do I avoid any type of risk?* When you're living an unlimited, fulfilling life in which you constantly <u>S</u>ee <u>N</u>ew <u>A</u>chievable <u>P</u>ossibilities, your answer will be a resounding *no!*

Can someone else take the credit for your life plan? Imagine that you're a little boy who really, really loves the arts. In particular, you want to become a ballet dancer. Baryshnikov is your hero. However, every time you pirouette across the living room or use the back of a kitchen chair as a makeshift barre, your father, who's a doctor, shakes his head and rolls his eyes. He usually follows up with a comment about how boys don't dance and *Why don't you think about becoming a doctor like me?*

It doesn't take you long to develop the belief that your father doesn't approve of your unique self, and that the only way to win his approval is to go down the path he has prescribed. (Baaaaad idea.) You become a doctor—and you can't figure out why the hell you're so freaking depressed every day of your life. SNAP out of it!

Granted, your circumstances might be different. Maybe you wanted to teach and your parents urged you do something "more lucrative," for example. Perhaps you wanted to start your own business but your spouse begged you to follow a more stable, less risky career path. The point is: Is your life proceeding according to *your* plan? Or someone else's? Whose beliefs are shaping your future?

Do you habitually play the role of rescuer? *Here, let me help you fix that proposal draft before you give it to the boss. Can I suggest a better way to use your tax refund? Sure, I can help make the PTA fundraiser more successful! You need to quit smoking, and I'm going to be with you every step of the way.*

No, there's nothing wrong with helping other people. But if you're constantly looking for folks to rescue, ask yourself why. Is it because when you're busy fixing others' problems, you don't have to do your own work? It's much easier to feel superior as you sit back and say, *Look what I've done for you!* than it is to own up to your own limitations and work to move beyond them.

Do you know what you love? If I were to ask you what you love (not people, but things, hobbies, interests, etc.) and you couldn't name at least three things off the bat, I'd say the odds are strong you're living in a restrictive box. Getting stuck at two, or one—or zero—things is more common than you'd think, and it goes back to fear-based noes. We're too scared to allow ourselves to pursue our true interests, goals, and passions, and instead choose to play it safe with options that don't excite us.

Feeling Uncomfortable? You're Not Alone.

If you answered these questions honestly (and are not, as Willy Wonka would put it, living in "a world of pure imagination"), you might be feeling uncomfortable right now. (The good news is, you're normal and this is a crucial step on the road to SNAP-ing.)

Now, before you turn the page, I'd like to ask you to take a few moments (or even a few days) to think about what you've just read. Look back through the assessment questions and come up with fuller, more thoughtful answers. See what new questions your answers spark. Discuss your thoughts and feelings with a trusted friend or family member, if you like. (Just be sure it's someone who's honest and who won't B.S. you to spare your feelings!)

Trust me, this isn't an "assignment" you can breeze through or skip if you want to get the full value out of this book. While SNAP-ing is powerful, it doesn't happen in a (forgive the pun) snap. Only when you put in internal work will you start to see exterior results.

"I'm through with playing by the rules
of someone else's game."
—From the musical *WICKED*

Chapter 2

Realize That the Boxed-in Life SUCKS

Are you still feeling off-balance after considering the questions I asked in the previous chapter? If you've really taken them to heart, you probably do. The realization that you're living a bubble-wrapped-and-double-boxed life can hit you on a vulnerable gut level. If you ask me, clearly seeing the box that surrounds you for the very first time is kind of like finding out that you've been living in the Matrix: What you thought was reality is actually an illusion. And the *real* reality sucks.

Why Don't We "Naturally" Realize That We Have Limiting Beliefs?

While you were unaware that you lived in a box, you probably never thought to question the beliefs and motivations that have shaped your life. Why would you? Like your height or your eye color, your beliefs that (for instance) you aren't very smart, or that you shouldn't question authority figures, have long been foundational, unchangeable "truths" you've lived by. And you have "proof" to back them up, don't you?

Let's start with "I'm not that smart." From your mediocre grades in school to the fact that you're never the team member who comes up with innovative ideas at work, there seems to be ample evidence that you're no Einstein.

And just look at what *always* happens when you disagree with a "superior." As a kid, your parents punished you for "talking back." Now, you get lectures and put-upon sighs from your boss when you question the status quo. (And let's not even talk about what happened when you asked your doctor if you could explore natural, integrative alternatives instead of being prescribed blood pressure medication.)

As time goes by, you collect more "evidence" that these "truths" about yourself are true. (Never mind the fact that the beliefs might be causing you to act in a way that keeps inviting such responses.) Your limiting beliefs become more solid and powerful over time. Sure, feeling like a dim bulb or a cringing underling may not be fun—but it feels normal. That's the thing about a boxed-in life. The walls grow up around you silently, sneakily, and unnoticed. And unless you receive a wake-up call (perhaps from a therapist, a clear-sighted friend, or dare I even say a book like this one), you have no reason to question your reality.

Seriously, Please Don't Beat Yourself Up About Not Recognizing Your Limiting Beliefs!

Trust me, no one wakes up one day and says to themselves out of the blue, *You know what, self? It's possible that I picked up the wrong belief about myself as a kid. My parents were tired, stressed out, fearful, and wanted to keep me close because they were overprotective. They probably didn't mean to send the message that I wasn't good enough or smart enough; they just wanted to keep me from getting hurt.*

There's no doubt about it: Realizing how your limiting beliefs have shaped your reality is a sucker punch to your psyche. What you may have assumed was a pretty decent existence has just been unmasked as a pale, passionless (and let's face it, probably pretty sucky) imitation of what your life could have been.

Now, for the very first time, you may find yourself wondering: *What might have happened if I had applied to grad school? What if I hadn't listened to my parents when they told me I could "do better" than my fiancé? What if I hadn't allowed my boss to push me into transferring to a position I wasn't excited about?* Suddenly, you're aware of crossroads, exit ramps, and alternate routes you might have taken along your life's path—and you're wishing you could have a do-over.

It's normal to feel regret at this point. (We'll talk more about how to manage and move past regret later in this book.) But right now, the last thing I want you to do is wallow in *could haves* and *should haves*. The past is in the past, and there's nothing you can do to change it. Instead, I want you to understand what your future can be like when you say SNAP Yes! instead of hell no. (Spoiler alert: Your future definitely won't suck.)

Just Jump, Dammit!

Every single day, life gives us opportunities to say yes. The farther these opportunities are from your comfortable box, the scarier they feel—and the more you want to say no to them. But saying SNAP Yes! can be great fun! Let me share a story.

Prior to my husband's recent birthday, I had been busy and hadn't planned anything special. (Hey, it happens. Don't judge.) So I said, "Rick, honey, why don't you tell me how you would like to celebrate your birthday? Anything at all, we'll go do it." Famous last words, am I right?

My husband got this really mischievous look on his face. (Okay, I'm being nice here—it was actually a diabolical look.) He then uttered one word: "Skydiving!"

My inner voice said, "Are you smoking crack? We are not jumping out of an airplane!"

But even as my mind's eye was picturing impending doom, I heard my outer voice say, "Yes, sure! Of course I will go skydiving with you!" (After all, I reasoned, this was my own fault for not proactively planning a couple's spa weekend. Live and learn.)

My husband was so excited that he immediately booted up the computer and booked a skydiving "adventure" for the upcoming weekend. Let me tell you, the next few days were a struggle for me. I was desperate to stay in my safe, earthbound box. It took all of my willpower not to sidle up to my husband and say, "You know, I've thought about it and I'm just not a skydiving type of girl. I don't want to jump out of a plane. You go without me!"

Hoping for some objective information to help me make my case, I started googling "people who have died while skydiving." But what I found out was fascinating: Skydiving is relatively safe! Only 1 in 100,000 people die jumping out of a plane, versus 1 in 6,000 while driving to work in the morning. (Maybe we should all just start parachuting into the office!) So I kept my mouth shut, and the weekend arrived all too soon.

Once our plane was airborne, I had a chilling realization: I was trapped in a metal tube with a bunch of crazy people. Here we were, preparing to jump into thin air thousands of feet above the ground, and my fellow passengers were laughing, high fiving, and arguing about who got to jump first. Soon, bodies were being sucked out of the plane's door—and these people were *still* excited. *What was wrong with them?*

All of a sudden, I heard my jumpmaster's voice: "Okay, DeDe. It's time to move to the back of the plane." *Oh hell no!*

In the most reasonable tone of voice I could muster, I said, "Wait, you mean where all of those people are being sucked out of the plane? No, no, I'm good right here."

Imagine my surprise when my body began involuntarily moving in the direction of the door. I looked down and realized that I was strapped tighter to my jumpmaster than a newborn baby is to its mother's chest. Frantic, I looked around for my husband. *Where's Rick? Where is he? I can't find him!*

Then I saw him. Rick was behind me, smiling and waving. *This whole skydiving thing was his idea, and he's letting me go first? So much for chivalry!* Just as I turned my head to yell, "You butthead!" I went flying out of the plane.

My first thought was, *DeDe, do not pee. If you pee, it will fly up all over your instructor. Short of death, that's probably the only way this situation could get worse.*

My second thought was, *Oh...hell...yes...I love this!* Yes, I absolutely loved the experience of skydiving. As I felt the air whip past my face, my fear fell away. I felt empowered, confident, and excited—like I could do anything. That, I realized, is the feeling of saying SNAP Yes! when you wanted to say hell no! It is the exact opposite of a bland, boring, unsatisfying, boxed-in, SUCKY existence.

Hold On to That SNAP Yes! Feeling.

Yes, I'll admit that in the grand scheme of life, skydiving is small potatoes. It isn't nearly as frightening or life-changing as ending an unhealthy relationship, making a major career move, or going back to school. But I think it's easy to imagine how absolutely amazing it feels to go from reluctance and terror to being surrounded by joy and freedom. That feeling is the "point" I'm trying to make here. It's what I want you to imagine when you envision life outside your box.

If you've ever been skydiving, maybe you recall the feeling I'm describing. And if parachuting out of an airplane is *not* part of your life's story, I'm sure you've had some experience where saying yes despite your misgivings and fears had wonderful results.

Have you ever considered that this positive feeling might not have been a fluke? That growth, laughter, fun, excitement, and fulfillment are all normal, natural results of saying yes to opportunities? Guess what? You're right. THEY ARE!

I'm not saying that SNAP-ing and leaving your box behind will be a journey filled solely with puppies, rainbows, and unicorns. In some ways, demolishing a lifetime's worth of limiting beliefs will be the most difficult thing you've ever done. But here's what I want you to remember: The unboxed life—the one you're working toward—*is worth it.*

So close your eyes. Let yourself wallow for just a moment in the general suck-itude of your colorless, voiceless, powerless, passionless life.

What are you saying no to? Where do you feel most pressured and restricted? Then take a deep breath and summon up that giddy SNAP Yes! feeling. Which one would you rather let define your future? It really is up to you.

"NOBODY GOT ANYTHING GREAT BY PLAYING IT SAFE."
—SHONDA RHIMES

Chapter 3

On the Other Hand, It Feels "Safe," Doesn't It?

We've established that living a boxed-in life sucks. But if you're like me—and most normal people—you might be able to hear a soft voice at the back of your mind whispering to you right about now. It's saying, *Sure, drop-kicking your box as far away as possible SOUNDS great. But is living in a box really such a bad thing? After all, think of the alternatives. If you take new risks, you could fail spectacularly—which might take your definition of "sucky life" to a whole new unbearable level. DON'T LISTEN TO DEDE AND HER FEEL-GOOD SKYDIVING SCHEME!*

I won't lie. There's a certain logic to that line of reasoning. There are definitely no guarantees in life. When we start making bold new choices, we increase our odds of making mistakes, right? If you transfer to a new department at work, you might find out—too late—that you don't have an aptitude for marketing, after all. If you join a writer's group, your fiction might be mocked mercilessly. If you paint your bedroom that bright chartreuse color you're drawn to (you know, the one that horrifies your mother), you might discover that she was right!

When faced with what-ifs like these, it's natural to want to stay in the box where—even if life isn't ideal or inspiring—it's familiar, predictable, controllable, and above all, safe. A bit of suckiness, you might feel, is an acceptable trade-off for security.

Allow me to disagree.

Here's What "Safe" Looks Like in Real Life.

Not too long ago, I delivered a keynote address and breakout session at a company's annual conference. I spoke about breaking through your limiting beliefs (basically, my presentation was this book distilled into an hour). Toward the end of the breakout session, I asked, "What do you want to do that you haven't been able to do?"

One woman responded that she wanted to run a half marathon, but kept stopping at mile eight. When I asked why, her response surprised me: "For some reason, I start thinking that people are going to say, 'I told you that you couldn't make it. You're not a runner.' And I lose my motivation to keep going."

"Who tells you that you can't run a half marathon?" I asked.

"Well, you know…people," she responded.

"Yes, but *who*? Your family? Your friends? Your coworkers in this room?"

No response. This woman couldn't name one person who was discouraging her from reaching this goal. Do you know why? Because she herself was the source of all her doubts, fears, and limitations.

When I asked who else had been unable to do something they really wanted for themselves, another woman stood up. She explained,

"I really want to help women who are underprivileged. But I don't have the financial resources or support to do it."

"Whom do you need support from?" I inquired.

"My husband." At this point, there were nods of commiseration and "mmm-hmmmms" from females around the room.

"So you've talked to him about your desire to help these women, and he said no way?" I guessed.

"Well, no…I haven't mentioned it to him."

"But you've asked other people for financial support?" At this point I had a pretty good idea of how the story was going to end, but I was hoping to throw this compassionate and intelligent woman a lifeline.

"Ummm, no. I've never actually gone out and asked anyone for money."

Now before you start thinking, *Oh good, I'm in the clear*, I would beg you to take a deeper and wider look at some of your own ridiculous justifications.

We all have goals, hopes, and dreams that never come to fruition because of our own limiting beliefs. We believe we're not good enough or smart enough; we worry that other people will think our plans are stupid. We're afraid to take a risk. (We might even be afraid of how our lives will change if we SNAP and succeed!)

How Does Fear of Success Hold Us Back?

In order to trade the life you live now for the life you think you want to live, something will have to change. *I won't be around the house to help as much, and my spouse won't like that. I'll have to figure out another way to get the*

> *kids from school to soccer practice. I'll have to move or at least downsize.*
>
> Change like that is terrifying—even if it's a necessary step toward achieving a larger goal! That right there will keep you in the box.

Whatever our reasons might be, instead of formulating a plan and putting it into action, we choose—consciously or unconsciously—to stay in a familiar place. We psych ourselves out before we reach mile nine. We neglect to ask for the support we need to make our dreams a reality. *That's* what safe looks like. And yeah, it definitely sucks.

DeDe Vs. Technology

Just so you know, I'm as guilty as anyone else of allowing my limiting beliefs to keep me in a safe-but-stifling place. One day I was sitting at the computer, attempting to make some updates to my email software. Soon I got stuck. I had no idea how to accomplish the next step in the process. So I called my husband over for help.

At this point, you need to understand that Rick is very technologically adept, and if he doesn't know how to do something, he just keeps digging until he figures it out. He likes the "language" of machines and gadgets. I don't. And somewhere along the line, I developed the belief that I *couldn't* figure out technology. I assumed that all but the simplest tasks would always be beyond me.

On this particular day, Rick said, "DeDe, are you serious? You can figure that out." Imagine his shock when out of the blue, I burst into tears.

"I just feel so stupid!" I sobbed. "I can't do this and I don't understand why you think this is funny."

Fortunately my husband has a good sense of humor, and he didn't take my outburst personally. After calming down, we talked about why I was so upset. I realized that my belief that I "wasn't smart enough" was something I just accepted as true. I also believed that I needed someone to tell me the "right" way to do technology. That was my safe place. I would much rather rely on other people for my technological needs than try to figure things out for myself…and risk confirming that yes, I really was that dumb.

Maybe you've guessed how this story ends. Once I stopped avoiding what I didn't understand and allowed myself to be still, I SNAP-ed. I successfully installed that email software update. I had to admit that feeling empowered when I sat down in front of my laptop was a lot better than remaining helpless in my safe (and sucky) place.

Yes, this is a mundane, everyday example. In the grand scheme of things, my email is really not that important. But the point I'm trying to make is *extremely* important. My self-limiting beliefs were not helping me or protecting me, as I had thought. They were holding me back, preventing me from learning and growing, and causing me unnecessary stress. The same thing is true for you—and will continue to be true until you leave the safety of your box and See New Achievable Possibilities.

What Are Your Safe Places?

Now it's your turn. What are your safe places? In which areas of your life are you accepting stagnation and suckiness in order to maintain a feeling of security? What beliefs and fears are keeping you stuck? (Your answers to the questions I asked in Chapter 1 should give you a pretty good idea.)

Here's a good litmus test to help you tell if you're boxing yourself up for safety's sake, or if a particular path forward is legitimately not a good fit for you. *Have you taken at least five steps toward making that goal a reality?* If you can't name five actions, you're probably stuck in the safe zone.

Let's look at an example: You're part of your company's product development team, and together, you've just finalized the plans for a new, improved Product 2.0. You have an off-the-beaten-path ad idea you'd love to share with marketing, but—of course—you're reluctant to step outside your comfortable box. *What if my idea isn't just unexpected, but unreasonable? What if they tell me to go back to my test lab and never come out again? Maybe I should just keep my mouth shut...*

If you stop here, you're guilty of letting your limiting beliefs keep you in the safe zone. Instead, I would challenge you to, as I said, take five concrete steps toward pitching your ad. For instance:

1. Draw (or Photoshop!) a mock-up of the ad.
2. Write a brief report describing the ad's intended audience and why the ad would appeal to this group.
3. Share your fleshed-out idea with other members of the product development team, your friends, and/or family members. Get their feedback and incorporate any suggestions that make sense. (Sharing your ad with a relatively friendly audience is a good way to warm up your "courage muscles.")
4. Practice pitching your idea to a live audience. Fine-tune exactly what you want to say and commit your pitch to memory.
5. Reach out to a leader in the marketing department and set up a meeting time. (Don't be late!)

If you've done all of these things, and a marketing decision-maker says, "Thanks, but no thanks," you've done your part. You SNAP-ed, stepped out of your box, and drop-kicked it impressively far from your safe zone. Your idea might not have panned out, but (I hope!) your self-confidence has grown. You've probably also learned some interesting lessons about marketing.

And hey—maybe the answer *won't* be no. Maybe that marketing decision-maker will say, "You know, you might be on to something here..." and go on to use part or all of your idea. The point is, you'll never know unless you take concrete steps toward making your dream a reality.

A Wise Voice

My voice coach, who is also a good friend, tells me that he's often more psychologist than teacher. So many students say they want to sing, but they don't practice. They don't look for opportunities to perform. They don't get on stage. They've recorded nothing. They have a lot of excuses for why they aren't singing, but it all boils down to one thing: *They've done nothing to make their dream a reality.* See what I mean? If you haven't done the basics to make changes in your life, *you* are the main thing that's holding you back.

The Ultimate Price of Safety

There's one more consequence of safety that I haven't mentioned yet, and it's the worst of all. If you choose to live a safe, boxed-in life, you will accumulate a crushing load of regret. It won't happen overnight.

You may not notice the presence of regret for years. But eventually you won't be able to ignore it—and it will have the power to destroy you. In the next two chapters, we'll be taking a close look at how regret can affect you—and how to move past it.

But for now, I want to end this chapter on a positive note. The bottom line is, your dreams are not there to haunt or taunt you as you gaze at them from the safety of your box. They're not supposed to make you miserable. They are tapping you on the shoulder saying, "You have the ability to create a life that utilizes your unique gifts and talents—you just need to step forward and take action." What will your decision be? I hope it's a big, loud SNAP Yes!

"Forget regret, or life is yours to miss.
No other road, no other way, no day but today."
—From the musical *Rent*

CHAPTER 4

R-E-G-R-E-T, Find Out What It Means to Me

The smart people who work at universities and research centers uncover some pretty interesting information about human nature and behavior, don't they? Of course, we give them plenty of material to work with! Many of us do and say things that are downright puzzling, even to the people who do and say them. But what is even more fascinating—at least to me—are the things we *don't* do and say. And that's why the study I'm getting ready to tell you about has really stuck with me.

In 2011, researchers from Northwestern University and the University of Illinois at Urbana-Champaign surveyed 370 Americans.[1] Unlike many previous studies on regret (which focused primarily on college guinea pigs…errrr, students), this one included respondents from many different socioeconomic and educational backgrounds. They ranged in age from 19 to 103. Each participant was asked to share one memorable regret—basically, what it was and how it happened.

As the researchers crunched their data, an interesting pattern emerged. The regrets that haunted people the most over time—the ones that refused to fade into the background—tended to involve something the respondents *didn't* do: an opportunity they failed to take advantage of, an action they did not take, etc. Regrets that centered around something people DID do—but wished they could take back—tended to be prompted by recent events. (In other words, short-term regrets are about things we do, but the regrets with real staying power are prompted by actions we DIDN'T take.)

That really rings true for me, and I bet it does for you, too. Of course, it's possible to regret an action for the rest of your life. I bet people including (but not limited to) the publishers who rejected the *Harry Potter* manuscript, Bill Clinton (I think we all know what misstep I'm referring to!), and the Trojans who decided to bring that horse into the city all *really* regretted their actions. But I think most of us tend to dwell more on what we *didn't* do than what we *did* do.

See, if you step outside your box and take a risk that doesn't pan out the way you'd hoped, at least you'll know that you tried. That particular score will be settled in your soul. (And/or, you'll know to never, *ever* do that again.) Once you get over the disappointment, you'll be ready to set off down an alternate path.

But if you *never* take a chance, step forward, or speak up, you will always wonder, *What if?* It's incredibly difficult to let go of the better future that might have been. It can be even harder to forgive yourself for playing it safe. Problem is, if you continue to fixate, ruminate, and beat yourself up, regret will take you down.

Regret in Real Life

What happens when a regret just won't go away? Sooner or later, it all becomes too much and you look for something—anything—to make that emotional pain go away. You try to numb out and shut down. And when you *succeed* in numbing out, you take your eyes off of your goals and vision, teeing yourself up for a whole new round of regret.

I know that type of regret—the kind that sends your whole life into a vicious cycle of bad decisions and even worse coping mechanisms. As a little girl, I always wanted to be on Broadway. (I know I've said this before—but bear with me.) Every night, Barbra Streisand, Judy Garland, and I would entertain adoring fans for hours on end. (Okay, they were stuffed animals who adorned my bed, but that's not the point.)

I didn't just dream about Broadway, either. I took the steps to make it happen. I took dance, acting, and voice lessons. I was in show choir, mixed choir, girls' choir, and Allstate choir. I was in all the junior high and high school musicals, won vocal contest after vocal contest, traveled to Europe on a singing trip, and even won a coveted vocal scholarship to the same college Broadway star Kristin Chenoweth attended.

But something happened while I was in college—something very different from what Kristin Chenoweth experienced. My fears got the better of me. I started doubting my ability. *I don't think I can make it on Broadway! There are too many other talented people out there. Why would a casting director choose ME over THEM?* (Now, I'm certain Kristin had many of the same fears—who wouldn't? But she stepped forward. She continued to say SNAP Yes! and take concrete steps toward her goals—and of course, we all know where her life is today.)

Soon, another mental voice began to chime in...and this voice sounded a lot like Bette Davis. *Oh DeDe, dah-ling, seriously! I know you were born to entertain, but how entertaining is it going to be when you are flat broke? When you can't pay the rent or afford to turn the heat on?*

Do you really think you can handle all of the criticism and rejection New York is going to throw at you? No. You're just not that confident, dah-ling. As for passion and purpose? Yes, I know that people talk about that all the time, but I want you to think bigger, DeDe. Think profit and power!

And I listened. I believed Bette. Bette must know better than me, right? I bought into the idea that a prestigious position and a high salary would not only make me *look* successful on the outside, but *feel* successful on the inside.

I have to admit that in my corporate sales career I *was* very successful. I did amazing things. But no matter how loud the accolades were, they could never drown out my regrets. Yet another voice popped up in my head, and it would not stop asking, *DeDe, why? Why would you listen to Bette over YOU? Why would you squander all of your talent and training?* Nothing could make those questions go away…until the day I met the rich, bold, dark Mr. Cabernet Sauvignon. And let me tell you, ALL of the voices in my head stopped, just like that.

For the next 24 years I carried on a close personal relationship with Mr. Cab Sauv and many of his friends. Yes, I was a three-bottle-a-night, blackout drinker. That, my friends, is just part—yes, I said *part*—of the price of drowning out the voice of regret.

You see, every day that I drank to keep my Broadway regrets at arm's length was a day that I did not turn around and face my fears. It was another day that I stayed in my box and did not take any steps toward building a fulfilling life for myself. I racked up 24 years' worth of days to regret staying safe. And by the time I finally said SNAP Yes! and decided to radically change my life, I had missed my Broadway window of opportunity.

Plus, I *had* faced plenty of other fears in those two-and-a-half decades. And with the 20/20 vision of hindsight, I could see that trying my luck on Broadway really wouldn't have been as scary or risky as I had originally thought. Even if I had eventually determined, *This isn't my path in life*, the world wouldn't have fallen apart. I'm pretty sure that at no point would I have been living under a bridge with no food, or been cast out as a social loser. And with that knowledge came a lot of self-blame and condemnation.

Talk about regret on top of regret on top of regret.

Regret Is a Tease…and a Liar.

In addition to beating you up with woulda, coulda, shouldas, have you ever noticed that regret is a big fat tease? When you do emerge from your self-induced numbness and allow yourself to think of things you wish you'd done differently, the alternate reality you imagine is always picture perfect. You see yourself as a complete success while ignoring the roadblocks, setbacks, and failures that *might* have happened along the way.

So personally—after I "officially" gave up on my dream, I used to picture myself as the Tony-winning lead in a runaway Broadway smash. (*I could have been Kristin Chenoweth, if only I'd stayed the course!*, I'd mentally moan.) I didn't imagine myself in a string of supporting, never-quite-in-the-spotlight roles. I didn't dwell on the fact that I might not have been called back to a single audition.

What about you? Do you picture your start-up idea as the next Apple (instead of another tech company struggling to survive)? In your mind, are you a Food Network chef (instead of a blogger whose intermittent posts don't get much attention)? A *New York Times* best-selling author (instead of the possessor of a pile of rejection letters)? A member of your company's C-suite (instead of an overlooked middle manager)?

Here's my point: Regret is the "gift" (from hell) that keeps on giving. It will paralyze you, divert you, drive you toward unfulfilling (or downright self-destructive) behavior, and keep you distracted from your goals and dreams. It will become an anchor around your ankles, and it will just keep getting heavier—UNLESS you SNAP, consciously choose to unhook from it, and let it go. (Releasing regret isn't as easy as flipping a switch—it's a process you must commit to working through—and that's what we'll talk about in the next chapter.)

Right Now, It's Time for Some More Soul Searching.

First, what do you regret? It's possible that something (or several somethings) popped immediately into your mind. But if you need a little prompting, here are some common sources of regret among people I've met:

- **Professional** (You stayed with the "safe" career field or position instead of the one that fired you up.)
- **Relationships** (You wish you'd handled your romantic life, family life, or friendships differently. Often, this centers around not cutting ties with hateful, critical, toxic people, or not spending more time with those you love.)
- **Education** (You missed an opportunity to further your education that might have opened up desirable opportunities.)

- **Finances** (You regret not saving, investing—or possibly spending!—more.)
- **Personal life** (You wish you'd maintained healthier habits, moved to another area of the country, spent more time on self-development, etc.)

Second, how are you keeping your regret at arm's length? What's your Cabernet Sauvignon? As I mentioned in the Introduction, substances like alcohol and drugs are *definitely* not the only way to stay numb. You might be distracting yourself from your regret through food, TV, video games, shopping, serial dating, or exercising. You might be striving for perfection or power. You might be running so fast you don't know what the hell you're running from—or toward!

Third, what is your regret preventing you from doing right now? I'm not asking you to dig up the past and rehash what you *might* have been able to do or accomplish if your regret hadn't happened in the first place. I want you to consider how today and tomorrow might look different if you decided to stop numbing out and refocused on what you *really* want out of life.

Your vision may not look the same as it did pre-regret. You might have to jettison some goals that are now out of reach, and you might determine that what fulfills you now is very different from what fired you up 10 or 20 years ago. That's okay. (Personally, I found that my Broadway dream had become a strong desire to educate, entertain, and inspire others—and that's exactly what I'm doing through my speaking and writing.) The point is simply to examine—probably for the very first time—how much regret is impacting you right now, every day.

Got your vision of a regret-free life firmly fixed in your mind's eye? Good. Keep it there. We're about to discuss how you can unchain yourself from regret and SNAP into the future you've envisioned. Can I get a SNAP Yes?

Disclaimer: There Is No Such Thing as a Completely Regret-Free Life.

Like many kids, I looked up to my uncle throughout my childhood. But if I do say so myself, I had an extraordinary reason to idolize Uncle Bobby: He was a real-life baseball legend. Yes, my father's younger brother was *that* Bobby Murcer: a five-time MLB All-Star who played 17 seasons between 1965 and 1983. Most of them were as an outfielder for the New York Yankees, where Uncle Bobby's teammates included Mickey Mantle, Thurman Munson, Roger Maris, and Reggie Jackson. From my early years, Uncle Bobby helped me understand not only the rules of baseball, but the value of teamwork, commitment, resiliency, courage, and more.

It's an understatement to say that Bobby Murcer used his talents and abilities to the fullest. He had a reputation for going after his goals with every ounce of his energy and focus, and because of that, he lived many of his dreams. In the world of baseball, he came very close to "having it all": success, money, the respect of his colleagues, and the love of his fans. But you and I both know that there aren't enough hours in the day or energy in our bodies to truly "have it all."

One of my uncle's biggest regrets was that his career took him away from his family. He was often on the road for six months out of the year. Looking back, Uncle Bobby wished that he had been able to participate more fully in his children's day-to-day lives as they grew up.

There were a lot of Little League games and dance recitals he never got to see and a lot of milestones he missed. He spent many evenings warming up in far-away stadiums instead of playing catch in the backyard.

My point is, even if you SNAP in a big way and drop-kick your box so far that you can barely see it, you will still have regrets. There is a price to pay for all of our decisions. But I know my uncle would say it's better to go out of this life swinging for the fence than just dreaming about hitting a home run—and I agree with him.

Endnotes

1   Parker-Pope, Tara. "What's Your Biggest Regret?" *The New York Times*, March 23, 2011. Accessed December 21, 2015. http://well.blogs.nytimes.com/2011/03/23/whats-your-biggest-regret/?_r=1.

"WE MUST ALL SUFFER ONE OF TWO THINGS: THE PAIN OF DISCIPLINE OR THE PAIN OF REGRET OR DISAPPOINTMENT."
—JIM ROHN

CHAPTER 5

Drop-Kick Your Regret

If you want to bust out of your box and say SNAP Yes! to the rest of your life, you have to get rid of the crushing load of regret you've been carrying. No, you can't bury it or ignore it or gloss over it. You have to drop-kick that regret so far away that it doesn't cause you emotional pain and distract you from your goals for the future. Only when you're Certified Regret-Free can you visualize new, fabulous ways of doing life and business.

Now it's time for the obligatory disclaimer, and (as always) I'll be up-front with you. Your regret didn't develop overnight, and it will take you longer than that to fight your way clear of its shadow. Maybe a few weeks, maybe a few months, maybe longer. And to some extent, you will be working to push regret out of your orbit for the rest of your life.

(Unless you figure out a way to live totally mistake-free…in which case, please tell me your secret!)

The good news is, there's a three-step process to help you win the battle with regret. The more frequently and diligently you work through it, the easier it will become. I call this process the Three Its: *Stop It, Lose It, Use It.*

Ready to drop-kick that regret? Can I get a SNAP Yes?!?

Step One: *Stop It*

Stop It! First, you have to stop telling yourself the story of your regret. You know my story. If it were a novel or a Lifetime movie, it might be called *A Broadway Dream Deferred*. After reading through the points I made in the previous chapter, your own regret story is probably fresh in your mind. Now, I'd like you to consider the place it currently occupies in your life. (As any good general, CEO, or mother of teenagers can attest, it's important to know your enemy.) These questions will help:

How often do you tell yourself your regret story? For our purposes here, your regret story could be either a chapter from your own history *or* the alternate reality that might have happened if it weren't for your woulda, coulda, shouldas. (For example, *I might have become a world-famous doctor if I hadn't followed my girlfriend across the country to this crappy small town.*) Over the next day or two, pay attention to how often you find yourself dwelling on your regrets. Are they regular intruders into your thoughts?

How much detail do you go into? Do you simply think, *Wow, I wish I had gone to grad school* and then move on? Or do you beat yourself up with a blow-by-blow replay of exactly why you decided not to send in your application and how gosh-darn *stupid* that was? Level of detail varies from person to person, and it's important to figure out where you fall on that scale. In general, going into more detail means that you'll have to make more of a concerted effort to *Stop It*.

My own regret story is full of vivid, life-like detail. I have a tendency toward self-blame, which means that I punish myself with excruciatingly detailed versions of things I wish I'd done differently. Removing my regret story from my mental playlist was a difficult habit to break.

How does your regret story make you feel? Regrets aren't exactly a mood-booster. After rehashing your regrets, you'll probably feel discouraged, depleted, lacking energy and motivation, depressed, and/or anxious.

Most of us are at the mercy of our emotions. We allow them to just drift over us and to stay as long as they like. We rarely stop to reflect on where they're coming from, how they're affecting us, or the impact they're having on our lives. And when you consider that your regret story might throw you into a crappy, unproductive mood for hours, its impact might be larger than you've ever thought!

Now that you know what you're up against, it's time to *Stop It*. First, acknowledge that the past is in the past, and that you can't do anything to change it. Actually say this out loud: "I do not have a time machine, and I cannot make my younger self behave differently." Remind yourself of this truth as often as necessary.

Secondly, figure out what triggers your regret story. Is it a person, place, or circumstance? I'm no advocate of avoiding your issues, but still, there's no need to taunt yourself with your regrets when you don't have to. For me, this means that I sometimes choose not to watch the Tony Awards because they make me sad and turn my stomach into a giant knot. Depending on my mood and mindset, I might choose to listen to a nice classic rock album instead of my favorite show tunes.

You may also find it helpful to designate a go-to regret replacement. Any time you catch yourself fixating on your regret, consciously switch mental gears and think of something else. Refocusing on a future goal is always a good idea. You might also challenge yourself to think of something you're thankful for right now, or you might simply picture something you love: the beach you visited on your anniversary, your dog, a pint of Ben & Jerry's.

Write It Down and Breathe It Out.

This exercise can work wonders in helping you *Stop It*. I highly recommend giving it a try.

First, get your regret down on paper. Transferring your thoughts from your head to a piece of paper (or screen) is incredibly therapeutic. Specifically, writing about your emotions can help you grieve the loss of regret. (Your regret story has been a major part of your life and will leave a void when it's gone. So yes, it *is* something you need to grieve before you can move forward and fill that empty space with more positive thoughts and feelings.) This is a technique used by many therapists to help people SNAP and move through their regret.

Work with the two main feelings that anchor regret: sadness and anger. Finish this sentence: *I am sad that...* List every single reason your regret makes you sad. Write until you can't write anymore. Next, do the same thing using the word "mad." *I am mad that...*

Here are a few examples:

- I am sad that I took my job for the money, not because I enjoy it.

- I am sad that I haven't felt fulfilled by what I've done for the past 15 years—years I can't get back.
- I am sad that I have missed out on a big chunk of my kids' childhoods.
- I am mad that I didn't have the courage to quit and start my own business after I paid off my student loans.
- I am mad that I have allowed my professional unhappiness to affect my mental and physical health.
- I am mad that I burned an important bridge with a potential investor.

Next, use your breath to release your regret. As you look over your list, allow yourself to feel the full impact of your sadness and anger. Do this where you'll have the privacy to sigh, cry, and even scream if you need to, so *not* on the subway or in the living room with your family! Depending on the length of your list, you might want to focus on only a few "sads" and "mads" at a time.

Then use deep breathing to loosen and release those negative feelings. As you inhale say, *Let*, and as you exhale say, *Go*. (Yeah, kind of like a certain singing ice princess.) Repeat this deep breathing and feeling exercise for a minimum of five minutes a day until you have felt all the sadness and anger recorded on your list.

You may think this exercise sounds hokey or ineffective. Do it anyway. I strongly suspect that you'll be surprised by how much better it makes you feel. Remember, great new things can't come into your business and life until you make space for them. And you can't let go of what you ignore or deny.

Step Two: *Lose It*

Now you have some tactics to push Stop/Eject on your regret story when it starts playing in your head. But how do you get rid of that regret tape (CD...mp3 file...whatever) altogether? You have to lose your excuses.

The longer you resist saying SNAP Yes! to life, the more regret(s) will pile up. (Remember, every day you stay in your nice, safe box is another missed opportunity to flourish and find fulfillment.) And what keeps us from saying SNAP Yes? EXCUSES! You know what I mean: *I'm too old. It's too late. I don't have the money. I don't have enough experience. I have kids. My parents need me to take care of them. I tried that before and it failed*...and so on and so forth.

Let's look at a short example. You want to lead a sales team, but each time an opening is available, you find some reason not to throw your hat into the ring. *I want to attend that seminar on prospecting, and it's not until next month.* Or, *First I want to become more confident at leading meetings, so I need more practice speaking to groups. I'll just stay where I am for another six months.* You want to know what you'll REALLY have a lot of after six months? It ain't a pile of life-changing experience.

It's a (big, smelly, steaming) pile of regret! The only way to lose the regret is to lose the excuses that are keeping you from stepping forward.

The good news is, we've already talked about how to lose your excuses. Excuses are how we justify our decision to stay in the safe zone, and as we discussed in Chapter 3, the only way to get out of the safe zone is, to borrow Nike's catchphrase, to *just do it*. I wish I could lay down some mind-blowing wisdom to help you lose your excuses without any discomfort, effort, or risk, but that simply isn't how life works. (Okay, hypnosis *might* do the trick…but if you wiped your memory of all regrets and excuses, wouldn't you basically be an amnesia patient?)

To illustrate the relationship between regrets, excuses, and action steps, let's return to my life story. We all know my "original" regret: *I could have been a star! A top-notch performer. A real contender in my craft.* As the years marched on, I added more to the pile: *I'm in my late forties. I haven't been seen. My voice might have deteriorated past help. What am I doing with my life? I'm STILL wasting my talent!*

I could have stayed right there in my box, marinating in the toxic mix of all my regrets. But I took a step out of my comfort zone and hired a master voice coach. I'm not saying it was easy or that I didn't have doubts—it wasn't and I did. But after a few coaching sessions, I found that one of my excuses had already bitten the dust: My voice had *not* deteriorated past help, and I still had a lot of potential as a singer.

Soon I was focused more on what I could accomplish *right now* than on what I had failed to do in the past, or why I couldn't get what I wanted out of life. As I continued to take more action steps, I was able to do some pretty amazing things, like sing the national anthem at a New York Yankees baseball game and an Oklahoma City Thunder basketball game. By this point, my excuses for not living the life I wanted were falling down like dominoes. And (surprise, surprise) as my excuses diminished, so did the load of regret I was carrying.

Here's the bottom line: Taking action steps dispels the myths that you create for yourself. What can you do right now to start losing your own excuses?

But What If I Have a Really Good Reason for Not Taking Action Steps?

What is holding you back from taking action steps? You may think you have a really good reason for staying where you are. But if I were sitting with you right now, I'd probably disagree. Unless there is concrete evidence that you will fail or that reaching your goal is not possible, you owe it to yourself—and your future—to do some further investigation. As long as you hide behind excuses, you'll also live under the tyranny of regret.

Your mission, should you choose to accept it, is to write down the reasons why you are not willing to step up, speak up, or show up. Your list must NOT include any what ifs, maybes, mights, or other hypothetical scenarios. For example, if your goal is to get a raise, your list should not include reasons like:

- I might make my boss mad.
- I might get fired.
- I could be a target when layoffs happen.
- Maybe I'm being overpaid now.
- What if my boss thinks I'm motivated only by money? I want to be seen as a dedicated worker.

Instead your answers must be an action step you have already taken, paired with a corresponding result. For instance:

- I asked for a raise last year, and I was told that no one would receive a raise until the company reached certain financial benchmarks. That hasn't happened yet.
- I have done the research, and according to industry standards a raise isn't justified.
- My supervisor gave me improvements to make in order to get a raise. I made all improvements on the list and my supervisor would not take action.
- I asked my supervisor what I would need to do to move to the next pay grade. In order to receive a raise in this position, I would need an additional professional certification—but I have no desire to spend time, energy, or money obtaining it.

Were you able to write down at least one road-tested reason (preferably more) why you can't move forward? If not, you're busted! Don't expect me to sympathize with your regret-induced misery if you won't even *try* to *Lose It*. Tough love, people.

If you *have* taken action steps toward your goal or dream and there is concrete evidence that what you are doing is not working, then it's time to look for another way to reach your goal. You may have proven that you aren't hiding behind excuses, but you can't give up now. If you stop Seeing (and working toward!) New Achievable Possibilities, you are setting yourself up for more regret in the future.

Continuing the "I want a raise" example, what are three alternative things you could do to get to where you want to go?

- Change positions.
- Go above superior to next level leader and ask for raise.
- Change companies.

Step Three: *Use It*

Remember how you feel when you're swamped with regret? "Like crap" is the answer to that one! You don't want to feel that way any more than you absolutely have to, do you? OF COURSE NOT! Thankfully, we humans can take advantage of a little something called *hindsight*. Since we know exactly how bad we'll feel when we pass up a great opportunity, we can use that knowledge to make better choices in the future.

The next time you're at a crossroads, the next time you have to make a tough decision, use your regret to help you move forward. Say to yourself, *I know how regret feels and I don't want any more of that for myself. I want to feel proud, challenged, and fulfilled.*

If there's one thing I've learned, it's that *fear* is almost always a better choice than *regret*. It won't be easy, but you can step through your fear. (And in reality, your fears are almost never as gnarly as you made them out to be in your mind.) You can devise a series of action steps to help you SNAP out of your box. You cannot go back in time and get a do-over to erase regret. Personally, I would much rather say, "Yeah, I gave it everything I had and it didn't work out the way I envisioned," than, "I wish I had just given it a try…"

So the next time your boss asks for your opinion…remember how regret feels, speak up, and be honest! The next time you have a great idea…share it with someone who can help you make it even better! The next time you wonder if you're good enough, strong enough, or experienced enough…find out! The next time someone asks you to go skydiving…say yes! The next time someone invites you out onto the dance floor…go!

> **You Can Also Use Your Regrets as Opportunities to Learn.**
>
> And, of course, you can use both regrets of omission (things you didn't do) and regrets of commission (things you did do) as pathways to personal growth. It's like your parents and teachers told you: Learn from your mistakes. If you regret how you handled a delicate conversation with a client, for example, examine what happened and figure out a better way to proceed next time. Never "waste" a regret.

Work It.

Working through the *Stop It, Lose It, Use It* process on a regular basis will keep you moving forward and will help prevent you from becoming mired in the past. Please remember, you *absolutely have to* face your regrets head-on if you want to bust out of your box and say SNAP Yes! to life. You can't make positive, growth-inspiring choices for yourself if your view of the future is blocked by a heavy pile of regret.

"If you can't see yourself doing anything else and you have the drive and ambition, get the training and go for it."
—Kristin Chenoweth

Chapter 6

Not Sure What You're Passionate About? You Owe It to Yourself to Find Out.

Let's talk about passion and why it's a must-have for saying SNAP Yes! Obviously, you can't See New Achievable Possibilities if you don't know what the heck you want to do once you bust out of your box. In order to build a life that energizes and inspires you, you need a clear vision to pursue, and if you want it to stand the test of time, that vision must be fueled by passion.

What Is Passion?

I define passion as living on your own terms, according to your own values, while pursuing your own dreams and goals. As such, passion requires constantly developing the courage to move past rejection and criticism so that you can be your authentic, talented, joyous self.

You can be passionate about many things: people, causes, places, activities, or certain kinds of work. (Very seldom is someone passionate about just one thing.) You might have some passions that are entirely personal and others that are purely professional. Often, you'll find a way to use your passion (for instance, helping others or improving existing processes) in both areas of your life.

For some of you, this won't be a problem. You'll be able to tap into your passion immediately once you step outside your box. But most of you are probably thinking, *Sure—SNAP-ing, living a fulfilling life, and leaving my regrets behind sounds great. But, DeDe, I don't really have passion. Nothing excites me. I can't think of anything that really fires me up or makes me want to forge full steam ahead into the future. I'm not even sure I know what that feels like.*

To that I say, SNAP out of it!

Maslow's Perspective on Passion

While writing this chapter, I reached out to my social media connections and asked how they incorporated passion into their lives. My longtime friend Garyld Miles, who used to be my high school show choir partner and is now the chief operating officer of The Realtime Group, sent me the following thoughtful response:

"In 1954, Psychologist Abraham Maslow published a book titled *Motivation and Personality* in which he suggested that all humans are motivated by a common hierarchy of needs, commonly displayed as a pyramid in which the most basic needs—physiological (air, water, food, and shelter)—are placed at the bottom. Once these needs are met, we gravitate to the second set of needs: safety and security. When we're convinced that these needs are met, we long for love and a sense of belonging. Then comes self-esteem. The highest aspiration, Maslow suggested, is self-actualization: 'What a man can be, he must be.' A teacher must teach; a painter must paint.

"But in his later years, Maslow added another dimension of needs at the top of the pyramid, a need even greater than and more rewarding than self-actualization: self-transcendence. This means going beyond our own needs and individual experience and giving ourselves to others. Maslow's final conclusion was that self-actualization is not the ultimate goal in life, but transcending self and focusing on others is."

What does this have to do with passion? Simple: Living with passion is the same thing as living a self-actualized life. It's making the most of your talents, strengths, and gifts. And, perhaps, the most passionate life of all is one in which we use those talents, strengths, and gifts to help other people and make our world a better place.

Garyld says, "It is this focus on helping others that helps to create a meaningful life…the more people you help, in big ways and small, the more it gets paid back to you…The more I help others reach their goals and objectives, the more my own personal goals and objectives are achieved."

> In a nutshell, human beings are hardwired to live with passion—it's our natural state!

No, Passion Is NOT a Silly Myth.

When I talk about passion, one particular objection almost always comes up. It goes something like this:

"Yes, passion sounds nice. It's a great buzzword to throw around when you're telling high school and college students to follow their dreams. You know, 'Find something you're passionate about and study that!' But in the real world, that advice is bogus. The most you can hope for is to find things you like and are good at. Passion is an overused, idealistic, meaningless word, and we need to stop acting like it's attainable for everyone."

Well, I think that's a cop-out. If you feel this way, it's a sure sign that you are consciously or unconsciously blocking your ability to live fully. I firmly believe that passion is part of the human spirit. You've just lived a double-boxed, bubble-wrapped life for so long you've lost sight of yours. Allow me to help you rediscover it.

What Stops People from Recognizing Their Passion?

If you do, indeed, possess passion, why on earth would you want to bury it? Easy: because your old friend Fear talked you into it. In order to live fully and authentically, you'd have to step up, speak up, show up, or grow up. You might need to let go of people or places, or have the courage to rediscover yourself. And you're not alone—many people have conditioned themselves not to feel passionate because they're afraid that going after what they really love will have unintended consequences or pull them in a direction they're afraid to go.

Here are the top 10 fear-based reasons why people don't live passionately:

1. Fear of going broke
2. Fear of being alone
3. Fear of being laughed at or criticized
4. Fear of failure
5. Fear of the hard work necessary to succeed
6. Fear of disappointing others
7. Fear of stiff competition
8. Fear of leaving their nice, safe comfort zone
9. Fear of having to confront painful emotions and truths about themselves
10. Fear of having to give up parts of their lives they enjoy

...And here are five more "bonus" reasons why people don't live passionately:

1. They think other people give a rat's ass about their life decisions. (Newsflash: Most people don't *really* care what you do, although they may find it fun to criticize you for their own enjoyment!)
2. They don't challenge themselves to think about what the first few action steps might be. (And if they do get started, they give up too quickly.)
3. They listen to bad advice from the "experts."
4. They aren't willing to carve out the time.
5. They never realize how good it feels to *just do it*!

There is real danger in running from fun, selling out, burying your talents, ignoring your natural abilities, and never setting fulfilling goals—basically, living a passionless life. You'll be really uncomfortable. You'll start to feel a low-grade anxiety that grows and grows. You'll become agitated easily. You may begin to experience various levels of depression. Eventually, to resolve your internal pain, you'll either disengage and numb out…or you'll step forward and do what you never thought you could.

What Are You Ordering Up?
Choosing to bury your passion is like voluntarily eating a microwaved burrito for lunch every day when there's a fantastic Mexican food truck just outside…giving away gourmet tacos for free! *I know what my order would be.*

What Can You Do to Find Your Passion?

First, stop thinking passion has to be some big, over-the-top thing. It doesn't help to pysch yourself out before you even begin. And once again, quit believing that you weren't born with passion or that you've lost it. Your passion is part of you—you can't just accidentally leave it behind somewhere like a phone or your car keys!

Honestly, finding your passion boils down to one simple thing: Start noticing your life instead of drifting through it with your eyes shut. But since I know you're probably hoping for a *little* more detail than that, here are some questions to help you get back in touch with your passionate side.

What's fun for me? No need to get fancy or sophisticated with this one. If teaching yourself Russian is your idea of a rip-roaring good time, fantastic! But "fun" could just as easily be playing laser tag, going to a comedy club, antiquing, or reading the latest FBI thriller on your couch. The idea is simply to identify things that you find interesting and that put you in a good mood.

What's easy for me? We all have things we just "get." Maybe accounting spreadsheets make intuitive sense to you (and fill you with satisfaction when they are completed correctly), but they frustrate your colleague to no end. Maybe you unerringly reach into the spice cabinet for seasonings that make your family and friends exclaim, "Sweet mercy, this food is DELICIOUS!" Or maybe you can always figure out how to put together furniture and appliances without cursing at the instruction manual for an hour.

What do I tend to "get lost" in? What puts you in a state of effortless flow? What can you do for hours on end without getting bored or losing momentum? Maybe it's painting, woodworking, baking, working on the minute details of your golf swing, writing, tutoring, or playing a musical instrument.

Personally, I get lost in decorating. It can be a single room, a whole house, or an outdoor deck or patio. I will arrange, rearrange, stand and stare for 20 minutes, then repeat the sequence for hours and hours and hours without stopping to pee or eat!

I also get lost in the process of producing videos for my speaking or singing career. I lose all sense of the passage of time, and my creativity just soars. Nothing distracts me from what I'm doing, not even my husband. There are many times I'm grateful to him for distracting me from work I *don't* love, but it pisses me off when he distracts me from things I'm passionate about!

What kinds of media do I gravitate toward? What kinds of books do you read? What magazines do you subscribe to? What types of online articles are irresistible clickbait to you? What do you like to watch on television? Look for commonalities, like an interest in history, medicine, fashion, cooking, politics, etc.

What fires me up? I'm referring to things that infuse you with excitement AND things that get your blood boiling. (Often, these reactions are two sides of the same coin.) Political views, social causes, and educational initiatives are all common answers here.

What do people say I'm great at? You are probably known for something specific amongst your family, friends, neighbors, and colleagues. Perhaps you're The Handywoman, The Party Planner, The Bargain Hunter, The Image Consultant, The Therapist, The Gardener, The Professor, The Financial Advisor, or The Car Guy. If you aren't sure what sorts of interests, skills, and strengths others associate with you, ASK!

Be Wary of Relying Too Heavily on Others' Opinions, Though.

It's fine to solicit others' opinions when you're uncovering your passions. Hopefully, there is someone in your life you can trust to push you, call you out on your B.S., challenge your answers, and encourage you to always dig deeper into what you really want.

But if you're expecting someone else to tell you what your passion is, then you need to SNAP out of it right now! Ultimately, no one knows what's best or most fulfilling for you but you. Think about it: Some people are passionate about flying through the sky at 60 miles an hour in a wing suit. But just because I'm a risk taker and like to skydive doesn't mean that I, too, want to become a human bird. No, I know what I think is fun—and so do you. The only question is, why aren't you doing it?

If I Could Support Myself Doing *BLANK*, I Would Do It in a Heartbeat.

What's your dream job? What would get you out of bed every morning, excited to start the day? If you could turn a hobby into a career, what would it be? What do you want your day to look like? When you were a kid, what did you want to be growing up?

The Value of Childhood Dreams

As a little boy growing up in Oklahoma, my uncle Bobby Murcer dreamed of becoming a New York Yankee baseball player. During his MLB career, even after being traded to the Giants and the Cubs, he never gave up hope of somehow making it back to the Yankees… which he did! Even after hanging up his jersey, Uncle Bobby wanted to remain an integral part of the team. So when he was offered the chance to go into the broadcast booth, he said SNAP Yes! and became an Emmy-winning sportscaster.

In his aptly titled memoir, *Yankee for Life: My 40-Year Journey in Pinstripes*, Uncle Bobby wrote, "For me there is only one team: The New York Yankees. That's been the case for me for more than 40 years. Truth is, and with all due respect to the Giants and the Cubs [to whom he was briefly traded] and to all the other teams I have watched as a broadcaster over the years, I'm blind to anyone else. One man, one team."[1]

I'll be the first to admit that Uncle Bobby is a bit of a rarity in that he was able to pursue the *exact* career he dreamed of as a kid. Most of us find that our childhood dreams were just a little unrealistic or uninformed, that we've grown out of them, or that life had other plans. But that doesn't mean our earliest ambitions can't help us find our paths and passions today. Dig a little deeper into what you wanted as a kid and why.

Take my father, for instance. His childhood dream was to play baseball. (Uncle Bobby told me that my dad—his older brother—was actually the better ball player!) But my father contracted encephalitis in high school, and his baseball dreams came to an end. Dad thought long and hard about how to deal with this cur-veball (pun intended) and carried his passion for being an instrumental team player into his firefighting career.

What about you? When you were a kid, maybe you wanted to be an astronaut because you loved the thrill of discovering new things. Maybe you wanted to be-come president so you could help those who didn't have voices to help themselves. Maybe you wanted to be an ice cream taster because quality was important to you. Maybe you wanted to be a park ranger because you loved spending time outdoors. See what I mean? I'll bet that a lot of the things you enjoyed and valued as a kid haven't *really* changed as much as you think.

What Are the Common Denominators?

Now, think about your answers to all of these questions. Maybe a few things stick out at you right off the bat. *You know, I think I'm passionate about blogging and volunteering to rescue homeless pets.* Or maybe you'll need to look deeper to see if there are any common themes in your answers. Do a lot of them revolve around teaching, connecting with other people, creating, or helping the environment? Trust me—if you pay attention, the answers WILL come. The trick is to look outside the box!

Remember you get to design your life any way you want. Do you want to work out of your house or in an office? Do you want to be a freelancer or have a monthly paycheck? Do you want to work part-time at a coffee shop or as a bartender? Do you want to be a speaker and accept only enough engagements to meet your financial needs, then spend the rest of your time doing volunteer work for the homeless?

What do you want to do? What do you have the skills to do? What are you willing to put in the time to learn? What are you willing to give up in order to obtain what fires you up? Basically, what kind of lifestyle do you want to live?

Why Raw Dog Food Comes to Mind When I Think of "My Husband" and "Passion"

(Yeah, I knew that headline would make you curious.)

My husband, Rick, worked in sales and sales management for 30 years. He wasn't passionate about his line of work, but he was effectively seduced by the money he made and the lifestyle he was used to living. (After all that's what you're supposed to do, right? Make lots of money, buy a big house, join the country club, drive an expensive depreciating asset, and go on lavish-but-not-really-that-fun vacations so that you can be part of the in crowd? Never mind the fact that you barely see your family, your health is deteriorating due to stress, and the people in the in crowd bore you to tears!)

Anyway, in 2008 when the financial crash hit, Rick was working for a hedge fund. It probably won't surprise you to learn that he was out of a job by 2009. But something about the money coming to a screeching halt caused him to SNAP! He made a decision that he was never going back to working for someone else. He wanted to follow his dream of being an entrepreneur. So far, so good.

To kick off this new era of being his own boss, Rick started doing something very similar to what he had done in his corporate life: trading stocks. He plugged away non-stop for four years. But for many reasons, being an independent trader wasn't what Rick thought it would be. Not least, he was tired of sitting behind a computer 24/7. So to get out of the house every day, he started a little dog walking business. It made sense: He had to walk our dogs anyway, so why not make a little cash, get some exercise, and renew his mind in the process?

Rick really liked his canine "clients," and he started wondering how else he could help them and their owners. The answer wasn't long in coming, because Rick is intensely passionate (Aha! There's that word!) about feeding our dogs a grain-free, kibble-free, all-raw meaty bone diet.

(I have been feeding raw for 15 years and had introduced Rick to this doggie lifestyle when we got married.) Soon, Rick was busy creating Raw Dog Food and Company, the business he now owns. Today Raw Dog Food and Company feeds Rick's soul *and* feeds dogs all over the state of Colorado (soon to be the country) a healthy, non-processed, one-of-a-kind diet.

Ricks still trades, but now he trades from a different, more relaxed perspective. He has taken the pressure off himself, and consequently, trading has become a lot more fun. His out-of-the-box lifestyle—a combination of trading and dog food!—is a perfect match made through a fearless searching of the soul.

My point? Sometimes it takes many steps to find that thing you really love doing. Sometimes you think you're going to love one thing only to find out your heart lies with something totally different. Sometimes you have to mix and match your interests in unexpected ways in order to discover the life you were meant to live. The key is to keep moving, keep observing, keep trying, and keep Seeing and believing in New Achievable Possibilities. In this way, at least, finding your passion really is a SNAP.

As we come to the end of this chapter, you may notice that I haven't directly addressed the big "but" most people have when it comes to passion: *But DeDe, my passion has nothing to do with my job. How am I supposed to SNAP and live outside the box when I feel stifled and unfulfilled at work?*

Good question. I'm glad you asked. The answer is so important that I've devoted the entire next chapter to addressing it.

Endnotes

1   Murcer, Bobby. *Yankee for Life: My 40-Year Journey in Pinstripes.* New York: HarperCollins, 2008. 213.

"My biggest talent is I know who is more talented than I am. I find them and I go to them and I learn."
—Liza Minnelli

CHAPTER 7

SNAP at Work? It's a Requirement for Success.

You don't need me to tell you that for most Americans, the majority of our adult lives are spent in our careers. Every morning when you peel yourself off the mattress and groggily get ready to head to the office for eight, ten, twelve, or more hours, this fact is glaringly apparent to you. Why am I reminding you of this depressing reality? Because honestly, the time you spend pursuing your profession *shouldn't* be depressing. And if you can find a way to tap into your passion at work, it *won't* be.

When you are getting paid to use your innate talents and abilities, you are happier, more creative, healthier, and more successful in all the ways that *really* matter. I've had the bookoo-bucks job, and I was never as happy as I am today entertaining, inspiring, and educating. Trust me: Bonuses and accolades will leave you cold and empty if you don't feel that you've fed your soul and made a positive difference in the world at the end of each day. (On another note, just because I'm using my talents doesn't mean there aren't any parts of my current career that I find to be a total pain in the butt. There are! Living passionately isn't the same as living *without* challenges; it just makes them easier to bear.)

Three Reasons Why Working in a Box Sucks

(No, I'm not referring to your cubicle here.) In earlier chapters, we looked extensively at why living your life in a box sucks. Just to refresh your memory, here are three quick reasons why your career won't satisfy or fulfill you if you stay in the safe zone:

1. Your box is a tight fit. (And the longer you've worked in it, the more bubble wrap and packing tape you've surrounded yourself with.) There's simply no room for growth and change. And without those things, you become irrelevant, replaceable, and shelved. That sucks!

2. Over the years you've made your box pretty comfortable—so comfortable that you've stopped taking risks. Whether you realize it or not, your courage and confidence are atrophying more each day, causing you to become increasingly anxious and fearful in our ever-changing business world. That sucks!

3. Great leaders know what their potential is. They use their experience, talent, and skills to make

> their businesses, communities, and economies
> more productive and resilient. They see change
> as a wonderful opportunity for success. If you
> are stuck in your box, you fail to see your value,
> and you're robbing the world of your greatness.
> That sucks!

First, let's get one thing clear about work and passion: Is there a preexisting professional position that will speak to every aspect of what you're passionate about? Honestly—probably not. I know very, VERY few people who would say, "Project management fires me up from my head to my toes!" or, "I can't wait to go to work every day and sift through supply chain management spreadsheets!" or, "As a salesperson, getting rejected by client after client makes me feel amazing!"

But you know what? I DO know quite a few people who might say:

- "Sure, I have to put out a lot of small fires and deal with some people who get on my nerves, but overall, I absolutely thrive on the challenge of planning strategically while building a strong team."
- "My company manufactures industrial cleaning equipment, which I really couldn't care less about. But I've always been an analytical person, and making sure our products get from Point A to Point B on time is like solving a complex puzzle. It's not uncommon for my coworkers to get frustrated because I'm so in the zone that I don't register the fact that they're talking to me."

- "Of course it's tough to be brushed off, rejected, and even insulted by prospective clients. But when I'm able to help a small business owner solve a chronic problem by utilizing one of the services my company offers, I really get the sense that I've made someone's life better and helped my local economy become stronger."

Do you see what I mean? You don't have to love every aspect of your job for it to still ignite *some* of your passions in *some* way, shape, or form. The problem is, too many people have gotten stuck or pigeonholed in a position that doesn't challenge them, inspire them, or make them feel good at the end of the day.

Need Help Finding Your Path?

If you're having trouble identifying how to tap into your passion at work, don't resign yourself to a lifetime of feeling stifled and uninspired. Often, we're simply too close to our professional routines, habits, and frustrations to take an objective look at how they might change. The good news is, there are a variety of tools that can help you figure out if you're in the right position, and if so, how to maximize your potential.

I'm a big fan of the Pathway Planner™ Assessment, an online personal assessment tool that will help you identify your unique strengths, talents, and abilities—all of which can provide insight into the career possibilities that may suit you best. While strengths and talents aren't always synonymous with passion, seeing where your skills might be an asset—especially if you never realized you brought a certain quality to the table—can help you connect your passion to your work. Research shows that when you find the right career match, you increase your satisfaction and level of success in a SNAP!

If you'd like my help in finding the right assessment for you or your company, visit my website to learn more: http://dedemurcermoffett.com/snaptitude-assessments/.

The good news is, you have choices. They may not even be as frightening or overwhelming to implement as you assume. While some professionals decide to go back to school, find a new employer, or even start their own businesses, many others find that there are viable and exciting options available from their current employers. Here are a few ways to begin changing your trajectory.

If You Want to Change Departments or Positions Within Your Company:

Maybe you've been making great money in sales for the last 15 years, but what really lights you up is working with numbers. Or maybe you're in a leadership position but you don't like babysitting other people. You want to go back into the more creative work of marketing. The following checklist will help you develop action steps to make your move:

- Get honest about who you are and what you want professionally. (The Pathway Planner Assessment I mentioned earlier can be a great tool to help you clarify these things.)
- Make a list of all the things you like and dislike about your current job. Be specific.
- Talk to a trusted peer in the position or department you would like to transfer to. Get a clear picture of the duties and responsibilities you could expect.
- Discuss with your spouse or partner what a professional change would mean for your relationship. Would there be a change in salary? Hours? Out-of-town travel?
- Write up your own reference or testimonial letter for why you would be great in the new position. You may never show it to anyone, but it will help you develop the elevator speech and talking points you'll need as you begin to move forward.
- Schedule a time to talk with the person who can make the transition happen for you. While your desires and well-being are important, make sure the discussion isn't "me-centric." Highlight how your company will benefit from utilizing a wider range of your strengths and talents. Many employers are happy to move a square peg out of a round hole. It's a win-win for everyone.

If You Want to Stay in Your Current Position:

You don't think that transferring to a new department or position is the answer—perhaps your current job really does utilize your skills and strengths. But at the same time, you can't deny that you're feeling frustrated, stifled, and/or disengaged. Consider whether any of the things you dislike at work might be within your power to change or positively affect. Think of it as SNAP-ing professionally. Instead of seeking out a new job, you're breathing new life into your old one.

When you make an effort to bust out of your on-the-clock box and engage yourself more deeply in your job, you can reap numerous benefits: A more efficient, effective, and rewarding workday; positive feedback from your boss; increased opportunities for development and advancement; better relationships with your coworkers; and (not least!) a sense of power and agency in your own life.

Here are some examples of how you might inject more passion into your workday (with the permission of your company, of course!):

- If the way you interact with customers feels shallow and scripted, innovate a new service process that allows employees to make a deeper connection.

- Create a shadowing program that allows employees to observe and learn from a colleague in a different department for a day. For example, external sales staff might shadow non-customer-facing employees, and vice versa. This initiative will promote interdepartmental understanding, communication, and service—which may promote an increased feeling of engagement across the company.

- Ask your supervisor if it's possible for your team to trade assignments periodically. Switching up the case study you're analyzing, the product you're promoting, or the prospect you're researching can get you out of a rut.

- Instead of keeping your head down, be more proactive in asking for feedback from colleagues and supervisors. You never know which piece of constructive criticism will help you take your performance and engagement to the next level.

- If you're bogged down by rigid procedures, incremental deadlines, and/or "too many cooks in the kitchen," ask where you might be able to carve out more autonomy.

- Spearhead a side project that enables your department or company to give back to the community. For instance, maybe you can offer your design services to a local nonprofit that needs help creating a website, or offer to provide free tax preparation to the needy. Feeling that you are doing meaningful work is an important part of connecting to your passion.

- Take advantage of any conferences, lunch-and-learns, and professional development your company offers. If you aren't acquiring new skills and challenging yourself, it's easy to become burnt out.

- Officially or unofficially, mentor a new hire. This may help you reconnect with why you chose your line of work in the first place and what you hoped to accomplish in your career.

- Look for a way to reduce costs in your department or organization. Perhaps the savings could be used to purchase technology, equipment, or training that will eliminate current sources of frustration.

- Disconnect from your laptop and smartphone as much as possible once you leave work. Being plugged in and professionally "on" at all hours is enough to make anyone lose their enthusiasm.

I would also like to share the perspectives of several people who have "been there, done that." Their strategies for tapping into your passion while staying in your current position may give you the inspiration you need.

Get involved in exciting, inspiring things outside of work. Passion outside the office can spill over to passion inside the office. Remember, if you're living in a box in one area of your life, chances are you're living in one in other areas as well. Drop-kicking any one of those boxes can jump-start a chain-reaction SNAP throughout your life.

Kate White, a *New York Times* best-selling author and former editor in chief of five major magazines, writes:

"When I was editor in chief of *Redbook*, there was a period when my work began to feel like a real drag. Around this time, my family moved next door in Manhattan to a woman who was one of the first female professors of geography in the U.S. She asked me one day if I'd like to go to the Explorers' Club with her for a lecture on Turkey. My kids were only 6 and 8 then, and it had been about six months since I'd had time to even shave my legs, let alone attend a lecture. But because I knew she might be lonely, I said yes.

"Well, that lecture *riveted* me. It also made me realize that since my kids were born I'd forsaken traveling, and I *missed* it. That lecture inspired me to start traveling as a family, on mostly offbeat eco trips, and all those experiences helped me like my job again."[1]

Volunteer for projects that scare you. While Liz Wiseman talks about applying for jobs that you don't think you're qualified for, her advice works just as well for taking on new assignments and side projects. Feeling out of your depth is scary, sure—but it's also exciting, challenging, and enables you to learn new things that may ignite your passion.

"I began to see that the best jobs are often the ones we're not 'ready' for. In our rookie state, a certain genius gets sparked and a learner's advantage kicks in. When we are stretched beyond our current capabilities, we can tap into a different mindset—what I have come to call rookie smarts—where we perform at our best and revel in the thrill of learning."[2]

Focus on the broader impact of your work. If you're worried that the sight of one more tedious form, email, or team meeting announcement will make you lose your mind, challenge yourself to think beyond those things. What does the form accomplish? Who will your email response help? How will the meeting move your team closer to its goals? On an even broader scale, how does your job contribute to your company's purpose of providing a good or service? How does your work impact our world? Pascale Witz says:

"I've spent 25 years of my career in healthcare, including GE Healthcare and now Sanofi. Throughout my career, I've found you have to focus on the broader impact of your work to stay driven and excited. In the healthcare industry, we develop medicines and solutions with the goal of ultimately improving the quality of life for millions of people worldwide. Every day, in everything I do, I feel that I'm working to improve people's health…

"I know my team is motivated by the work that we do and how it could eventually help a patient manage a chronic condition, like diabetes, or prevent an epidemic, like dengue fever. Of course, keeping motivated is not a given, even when you work in the healthcare industry. You can get diluted by daily processes or frustrated by setbacks, especially when performing activities that do not seem directly linked to helping patients. In this context, it is extremely important not to lose sight of our larger goal—helping patients. This focus on changing lives for the better and motivating people working toward that goal are definitely a driving force for me."[3]

Finding your passion at work doesn't have to be brain surgery (but sometimes, it is!).

My friend Giancarlo Barolat, MD, is an accomplished neurosurgeon who currently practices neurosurgery and neuromodulation in Denver, Colorado. He wrote the following reflections on how passion steered him into his chosen career—and how it continues to motivate and drive him.

"For the past 40 years I have been lucky to have been involved with an activity that is at the same time my day job, my passion, and my mission. My decision to become a neurosurgeon was not made because of financial, career, or lifestyle considerations. In particular, two events changed my life and determined the course of my professional career.

"The first occurred while I was in medical school, determined to become a psychiatrist. In my last year of study, my father had a massive stroke. He was admitted in a coma to a neurological ward where he died two weeks later. I attended my father every day, interacted with the neurologists, and learned about the complexity and mysteries of the nervous system (by far and large still a vastly unexplored territory!). I was touched on an extremely personal level by my father's affliction, and I was intellectually stimulated by the challenge of tackling a vastly un-charted discipline. I thought that by becoming a neurosurgeon I could diagnose pathological conditions of the nervous system, but I could also potentially eradicate them and cure them.

"The second life-changing event occurred when I was 26 years old and a resident in neurosurgery at the University of Torino, Italy. I was privileged to be involved with one of the first surgical implantations of a pacemaker-like device on the nervous system. Through that procedure, I was able to help a hopeless young woman who had been paralyzed by a severe motor vehicle accident. That was it! A light bulb went off in my brain! *If I can combine my knowledge of the nervous system with this newly discovered implantable computer chip technology, I can really break new grounds and help otherwise hopeless individuals.*

"And that has been, ever since, the theme of my life: relentless pur-suit of scientific evidence and methods to help unfortunate individuals who have been affected by various disabling conditions of the nervous system. A vast majority of the individuals I have helped and still help are affected by severe, incurable, devastating pain. They have been through all the treatments available and are still tortured 24 hours a day. Some of them have considered or attempted suicide. Some are adults and others are in their teen years, all with no prospects ahead of them but a life of pain. By spending countless hours studying the nervous system and developing new technologies, I have been able to put a smile back on the faces of many of these patients. And that is the best feeling in the world. It has propelled me through countless difficulties over the past 40 years.

"Of course, technology alone is not enough to fully heal, if one does not also pay attention to the emotional side of the issue. As I always explain to my patients, there are two different facets to pain. One is the 'pain' itself, which is a sensation (albeit a very unpleasant one), just like touch, heat, cold, or pressure. The other is 'suffering,' which encompasses all the emotions, lifestyle changes, and psychological issues that are created by the pain sensation. Defined in this way, suffering often ends up being more devastating than the pain itself. Alleviating pain without paying attention to the consequences of suffering gets the job only half done. I have found that it is necessary to take a much broader approach to treating the patient: establishing a relationship based on mutual trust, respect, and love.

"I feel fortunate that I have found a meaningful calling that allows me to make a substantial difference in people's lives, make a dignified living, and satisfy my intellectual and scientific curiosity. I am the luckiest person in the world.

"The same principles, of course, can be applied to any activity or career path. Follow your passion and fully immerse yourself in your profession. Do what is good for humanity. Money, success, and recognition will most likely follow. In any case, you will gain tremendous personal rewards that will fill your life with joy and accomplishment."

I'm sure Dr. Barolat would have built a satisfying and successful career if he'd stuck with his initial goal of becoming a psychiatrist. However, he was able to turn a career into a true calling by finding the courage to SNAP in his last year of medical school—while also grieving his father. Changing trajectories at that point was certainly daunting, and I'm sure it didn't exactly feel safe to Dr. Barolat. But because he boldly stepped out of the box, Dr. Barolat can now look back on a life he loves, knowing that he has made a positive impact on the lives of many.

This SNAP Isn't Optional.

Tapping into your passion and finding engagement at work is the SNAP on which all other positive changes depend. Why? As I've pointed-ed out, you spend at least 40 hours at work each week (and probably more). If you settle for disengagement and mediocrity in this area of your life, chances are you'll never fully bust out of the box in other areas.

No matter what your age is or how long you've been on your current career path, it's never too late to change your attitude, your actions, and perhaps even your job description. Trust me on this—remember, I spent over 25 years in a field that didn't resonate before I finally stopped numbing out and started pursuing the life I wanted.

So be patient. Take small steps forward. If one of the strategies I've shared doesn't seem to be helping your disengagement, try another. Just don't make the mistake of believing that simply surviving your job is enough. You CAN earn a paycheck while also fulfilling yourself intellectually, emotionally, and even spiritually. In fact, you deserve a life and a calling you can feel passionate about—whether you're a brain surgeon (like Dr. Barolat), a professional motivator (like me), a butcher, a baker, a candlestick maker…or whatever title is on YOUR business card.

The bottom line is this: Money won't do it, status won't do it, and accolades and awards won't do it either. The only way to make this life as full and rich and wonderful as everyone dreams for it to be is to understand that your actions, your thoughts, and the work you do can and should make a difference—to you *and* to other people. Remember: You change lives. You are important. You impact the world. You are needed. You are IT! Can I get a SNAP Yes!?!

Endnotes

1   White, Kate. "How to Cure Low Job Libido: Advice from Kate White." *Forbes*, July 2, 2013. Accessed January 28, 2016. http://www.forbes.com/sites/dailymuse/2013/07/02/how-to-cure-low-job-libido-advice-from-kate-white/#6cce985f4de5.

2   Wiseman, Liz. Quoted in Gina Belli. "The Best Way to Stay Excited About Your Work: Take a Jon You're Not Quite Qualified For." *PayScale*, November 23, 2014. Accessed January 28, 2016. http://www.payscale.com/career-news/2014/11/the-best-way-to-stay-excited-about-your-work-take-a-job-you're-not-quite-qualified-for.

3   Witz, Pascale. "How do you stay excited about your job?" *Fortune*, November 13, 2014. Accessed January 28, 2016. http://fortune.com/answer/pascale-witz-evp-of-global-divisions-at-sanofi-shares-how-she-stays-excited-about-her-job/

"You decide you will wait for your pitch. As the ball starts toward the plate, you think about your stance. And then you think about your swing. And then you realize the ball that just went by you for a strike was your pitch."

—Bobby Murcer

CHAPTER 8

Stop Being a Box Bargainer

Freedom of choice is awesome. You really do have the option to build your business and life any way you want so that it reflects your passion and your values. But here's the thing about SNAP Yes! choices: They never stop coming at you. You will never reach a point where you aren't asked to choose between fear and regret as you pursue the life you want. It will never *not* be necessary to take bold action steps into the unknown. You will never get a 100 percent guarantee that the path you're on will take you exactly where you want to go. You will never feel entirely comfortable and safe.

This constant bombardment of scary choices (and the temptation to bury it all under the relatively risk-free status quo) is, I think, what tends to keep people from following through once they begin to SNAP. We could handle one or two (maybe even nine or ten) big decisions a year, but most of us are faced with a crap-load more than that. It's stressful and exhausting to constantly wonder if you're doing the right thing. *Where's my crystal ball, am I right?*

And all the time, your box is right there in your peripheral vision, trying to lure you back to safety. The farther away from the box you are, the more likely you are to see only the comfort zone it represents, and to ignore the sucky-ness and stagnation it inevitably causes.

Eventually you will want to succumb to the lure of your box and return to that safe space. This may happen after one uncomfortable action step, or after 100. It might take a week after you decide to SNAP, or a decade. Sure, you'll still feel your dreams and your passion tapping you on the shoulder. You'll still have the talent, desire, and ability to create the positive life you want. But you'll think to yourself, *Couldn't I have the best of both worlds—safety AND happiness? Would it be possible to live with one foot in the box…and one foot out?*

When you start playing this game, you, my friend, become what I call a "box bargainer." And I'm sorry to burst your bubble, but box bargaining just doesn't work.

Let's Take a Moment to Clarify.

To be totally clear, box bargaining is different from the initial process of busting out of your box. Box bargaining happens *after* you've said SNAP Yes!—even if it was only a little bitty SNAP. As you move away from your comfort zone, you start feeling nervous that you've made the wrong decision—so you put "just one foot" back into the box. Living with one foot in and one foot out is your bargain.

Characteristics of the Common North American Box Bargainer

What, exactly, do I mean by box bargainer? If you've ever been on a diet, you probably know exactly what I'm talking about. *Yes, I will eat healthy and lose those extra 20 pounds…starting right after I eat this bowl of Cherry Garcia ice cream.* (Fun fact: This delicious Ben & Jerry's flavor is my own personal favorite!)

Box bargainers are the alcoholics who say, *I'll drink only beer instead of hard liquor.* They're the moms who swear that they'll stop and really listen to their kids…right after they get the house cleaned, the laundry done, the yard mowed, and dinner ready. They're the workaholics who promise to spend more time at home as soon as *this one big project* ends. They're the unhappy employees who vow to make a change when they're just a little more financially stable.

Box bargainers talk a good game. They know the right things to say, because at some point, for some length of time, they've succeeded in living outside the box. However, fear—of criticism, rejection, mistakes, and failure—has gotten the better of them. (It has caused them to "un-SNAP," if you will.) They are crippled by uncertainty. They'll move a short distance from their box—maybe that's voicing their opinion, or making a change to their established routine. But as soon as they are hit with pushback, they retreat instead of forging ahead. It's one or two steps out of the box, then right back inside.

Often, these individuals become addicted to the never-ending game of bargaining. It's way easier than saying, "Damn the torpedoes," pulling the trigger, and actually doing something different. Box bargainers' minds overrule their hearts. Their limiting beliefs anchor them in their boxes more than their passions pull them out.

Sound familiar? If it doesn't yet, it will eventually. You need to remember that while box bargaining might *seem* like an acceptable strategy, it doesn't allow you to be fully alive. Nor does it allow you to See New Achievable Possibilities in your career and personal life.

Are You a Box Bargainer?

It's tough to take an honest look in the mirror, especially when you're trying to identify characteristics and behaviors that could use improvement. You may be legitimately unsure of whether you've fallen into the box bargaining trap, or you're just experiencing the normal growing pains of saying SNAP Yes! to the next stage of your life.

The following red flags are common among box bargainers and may help you determine if you belong in this category:

- You constantly agree with others just to get along and to avoid rocking the boat, not because you're on board with what has been said.

- You shy away from stepping forward and voicing your opinion. At the same time, you wonder why no one listens to you or seems in tune with your needs.

- You can't handle rejection or criticism. Any type of pushback triggers your flight response, not your fight response.

- You're experiencing anxiety and depression. This can happen because every time you return to your box, you reinforce the notion that life is difficult, that you're not good enough, etc. That's enough to make anyone's mental health begin a downward spiral!

- You habitually delegate authority to others. Be aware that "delegating authority" can mean allowing another person to choose *your* opinion, the best course of action, etc.
- When there's conflict, you're usually the first to back down. Of course we all have to compromise and even give in from time to time, but when doing so becomes your default, you'll begin to feel invisible and worthless (which don't exactly accelerate the SNAP process).
- You feel jealous—not supportive of or inspired by—others' success. Often, this comes from knowing that you have the ability to achieve similar success for yourself. You just don't have the balls…and that pisses you off! (More on balls soon. Yes, really.)

The Cost of Bargaining

Now, let me share a story about how restrictive box bargaining can be…and how drastically your life can change once you stop the cycle. I have a friend—we'll call her Evelyn—who works in sales. It was very important to Evelyn that her kids have a parent present at home when they were not in school, so she began working from home after her children were born. (Her husband, a stock broker, continued to work outside the home.)

A little clarification here: When I say "work from home," I don't mean that Evelyn put in a few hours a day in a nice home office. She worked as many hours as she could from her dark, dank basement because that was the only free (and relatively quiet) space in the house. This setup wasn't ideal, and Evelyn hated it—but she kept plugging away because she is a professionally driven woman who is fulfilled by her career. "This works for my family, and I'm the only one who's suffering," she would say. "Being isolated in my crappy basement is better than quitting my job or upending my family life so that I can take a different position."

In other words, Evelyn was bargaining. By finding a way (albeit a less-than-ideal way) to continue working while mothering, she was taking an action step toward the life she really wanted. However, fear was keeping her from SNAP-ing and taking the additional steps needed to truly be happy.

Eventually and inevitably, Evelyn reached a breaking point. "DeDe, I'm so depressed," she told me. "I feel like I'm a short step from becoming suicidal. I'm drinking all the time because I'm so miserable. I'd love to be in outside sales but I just don't know if that's an option."

Seeing this as a possible SNAP moment, I told Evelyn in no uncertain terms that her unhealthy bargaining had to stop. I encouraged her to take the next step. "Talk to your company, tell them where you are, and ask if they can offer you any alternate options. If not, you're no worse off than you are now. But maybe you'll be surprised."

Wouldn't you know it, Evelyn's company jumped at the chance to have her as an outside salesperson. They offered her a great new position—but it had a catch. She and her family would need to move from Texas to California. Evelyn would be traveling often, so it would be her husband's turn to be home more often with the kids. Evelyn could have jumped back into her box at this point, but she didn't. She refused to bargain anymore, and she and her family moved to California.

The transition wasn't easy. (Putting more distance between you and your box never is.) Evelyn and her husband had to renegotiate their roles within the family, and for a while, *he* was depressed as hell! Fortunately, Evelyn's courageous example inspired him to SNAP, too. He moved away from the trading world (which he was never that passionate about anyway) and is exploring an entrepreneurial path that's in line with his marketing degree.

Thank goodness Evelyn didn't go back to her box after taking that first step forward. There were certainly many reasons *not* to move, and she received a lot of pushback. However, she insisted that this was something she needed to do. She was conscious enough to see that she wasn't being a good mom, spouse, or employee, and that she was going to drown if she continued to bargain with her happiness. Today, she says she has never felt more alive.

You Need Big Balls of Courage.

The only way to stop being a box bargainer is to grow big balls… of courage! I had to. Evelyn had to. Steve Jobs had to. J.K. Rowling had to. Donald Trump had to. (Well, maybe The Donald was born with them…) Every successful, fulfilled person on this planet has had to grow big balls of courage. The question is, how? Turn the page and you'll find out in a SNAP!

"WHEN YOU COME TO A FORK IN THE ROAD, TAKE IT."
—YOGI BERRA

CHAPTER 9

Do You Have Big Balls... of Courage?

Everyone talks about courage and confidence like they're qualities you can snap your fingers and instantly possess. That's not the way it works. Before you can grow your courage, you have to have something you're afraid of. Before you can grow your confidence, you have to have overcome that fear by feeling it and facing it anyway. That's how big balls of courage are grown. Fear first, feeling second, finding out you will survive third, and fourth, repeating that process again and again and again.

When you start living outside the box, your balls might be small, but they'll grow when you see that other people's opinions won't kill you, and that swimming against the current makes you stronger. The payoff of developing big balls of courage is that you get to live a happier, more fulfilled life according to your beliefs and values. *Can I get a SNAP Yes!?*

Forget the Box of Chocolates. Life Is Like...a Roller Coaster.

Learn to view life as a roller coaster that you must remain strapped into if you want to arrive at the land of your dreams. Think about it. The first time you ride that roller coaster you are going to scream your lungs out and almost throw up your lunch. But over time, the ups and downs no longer scare you or even make your palms sweat. You have faced your fear over and over again, and now you can ride that thing with your hands up screaming for fun instead of from fear.

Before long, you'll be bored by this roller coaster. Then it will be time to seek out another one that will allow you to feel that rush of fear and remind you just how alive you are.

How to Go from Boxed-in to Big Ballin'

Allow me to share some guidance that will help you feel and face your fears as you work on growing the biggest balls of courage you've ever had. (Yes, some of these tactics overlap with advice I've already given you. Get over it. This stuff is important, SNAP Yes! it is, and a little review never hurt anyone!)

First, admit that you are boxed in. It's simple: You can't make a change until you admit to yourself that you need to SNAP, or that your SNAP-ing has stalled (I'm looking at you, box bargainers).

Be conscious of how you feel. Give some thought to what makes you feel happy (or not), what makes you feel heard (or not), and what makes you realize you're living up to your potential (or not). The courage to make meaningful change begins with an awareness of how you feel.

You don't have to take your emotional temperature every five minutes; I'm talking about a bird's-eye view. As you go through the day or week, don't you know if something isn't right? Of course! It eats away at you and invades your life. That feeling is where the addictions, disorders, taking on too much, and other numbing-out behaviors come from. Try to identify its source or sources so that you'll know where to focus your efforts.

Ask what you can't live with anymore. Whether you've never SNAP-ed or are a habitual box bargainer, chances are your boxed-in life manifests itself in multiple ways. For example, if you share your opinions with your more placid coworkers but keep them to yourself when more dominant personalities are in the room, it's also likely that you censor yourself with certain friends and family members.

Trust me, it will be exhausting and overwhelming to tackle everything at once. Start by going after the low-hanging fruit. What can't you live with anymore? What habit would be easiest to change? What would cause the most positive improvement throughout your life? Is it something "big" and "obvious" like the career path that stifles you, the spouse you no longer have anything in common with, or the city you hate? Or is it something subtler, like a character trait or behavior that tends to sabotage your happiness? (This is one area where being in touch with your feelings comes in handy!)

Create a plan. We've talked about action steps before. You need them to bust out of your box in the first place. You need them even more if you are trying to quit a box bargaining habit. Why? Because box bargainers know what that outside-the-box, "I'm skydiving!" feeling is like, they are often more inclined to rush ahead without proper preparation. They are so eager to reach the payoff that they don't put enough thought into how to get there.

Don't Leap Before You Look.

Many people confuse courage with blind faith. Yes, there are times when we will have to take risks without knowing what the outcome will be. But when it comes to changing your life financially, I highly recommend having big, wide-open eyes before you jump. Today there is no shortage of people and companies selling you on the dream: *For just $29.99 you too can live financially-free AND worry-free! Just follow my 10…oh heck, make it my 3 easy steps and you will go from enduring to ecstatic in a SNAP!* Well slap me silly and sign me up!

Oh, come on, people. You know life doesn't work that way. Anything substantial you do is going to require hard work. Any major, SNAP-tastic path you take is going to be fraught with roadblocks, setbacks, and failures. I'm not saying don't take chances; I AM saying fully investigate the pros and the cons of your new venture before forging full-steam ahead.

I know this from personal experience. As I've mentioned before, prior to the 2008 economic crash, my husband, Rick, worked for a hedge fund. He didn't love what he was doing, but he endured. His rationale was, *Right now, my paycheck and the security it provides is worth staying where I am.* After the hedge fund took a big hit in 2008, Rick was finally ready to move toward other opportunities. He was passionate about becoming an entrepreneur, so he jumped into independent stock trading.

Don't get me wrong; Rick worked like a dog. For several years, from sunup to sundown, he studied and went to seminars and put in ungodly hours. But to make a long story short, Rick couldn't fully understand the volatility of what he was getting into, or how risky being an independent trader really is, until he transitioned from studying to doing. Turns out, the trading gurus don't tell you that you will likely lose a substantial amount of money as you build your business. Most people don't have the finances to withstand those kinds of losses.

In hindsight, we both learned a big lesson: Overzealousness, combined with naiveté and a fear of not having an income, can drive even the smartest of people in the wrong direction. Happily, as you know, this story ends positively. But make no mistake, the consequences of leaping before you've looked can be lasting and

> life-changing—and not in a good way. If you go too
> many miles in the wrong direction, it's very difficult to
> get back on track. Use your time wisely—don't let time
> use you.

Make sure that you have a well thought-out action plan in place as you move away from your box and/or stop bargaining. Take time to investigate the feasibility of the changes you want to make. Do you have the financial, energetic, and emotional resources to get from point A to point B? What's a realistic timeline? How will moving toward your passion impact the rest of your life? Are there any changes or compromises you should prepare for (e.g., downsizing your home, changing your schedule, etc.)?

Don't make your action plan so detailed that you work on it forever and never actually get started—but do make sure it *is* a plan, and not just wishful and idealistic thinking. Also, make sure it's a plan that exists in concrete form, not just in your mind. List out the action steps you will need to take. Maybe even make a vision board that creates a visual, emotional connection to each action step, if that's your thing. (Heck, build a PowerPoint presentation if you're feeling really fancy!) Sure, your plan will change as you move forward. But with each step, you'll find out more about whether this is what you really want, how feasible it is, and how best to get there.

Keep yourself accountable. You already know that your box will always be in your peripheral vision, tempting you to return to your safe zone. You stand a much greater chance of resisting that temptation when you have teammates to support you and call you on your crap when necessary. Trust me on this. As a speaker, everyone in each of my audiences is an accountability partner. Many will go out of their way to thank and encourage me, and I urge them to call me out if they see that I'm not walking my talk.

Find a few people you trust—friends, family members, coworkers, mentors, etc. I suspect you'll be pleasantly surprised by how many people want to help you (and you never know who is connected to whom). Explain to them the changes you want to make and why it's important that you not return to your old ways. Familiarize them with your action plan, take into account any helpful feedback they give you, and keep them posted on what's happening as you move forward.

Maybe you'll want to set up formal accountability meetings, or maybe you'll simply chat about your progress over the occasional coffee. Do what works for you. (Be honest. You know if you're the type of person who needs more oversight and encouragement, or less.)

Find a few (realistic!) role models. Seek out others who have walked similar paths to the one you're setting out on, and who have successfully drop-kicked their boxes. Ideally, this group will include someone you can interact with semi-regularly. Be sure to consider on-line groups when looking for role models if you don't know a suitable candidate personally. There truly is a community for everything—you are never alone in the life you want to leave behind. Especially thanks to social media, it's never been easier to find people who are working toward the same thing and are willing to share advice.

I do have one caveat to share: Make sure your role model sets a realistic example that you can follow. In other words, he or she shouldn't be too far "above" you in achievement level. If you've ever lost weight, you probably know what I'm talking about. It's much easier to connect with a friend who has just lost 20 pounds and is still in pursuit of his goal weight than it is to connect with an uber-ripped celebrity fitness guru. One represents a level of achievement that feels within your grasp;

the other might make you sigh, "I'll never look like that. Why am I even trying?"

Change the venue. If you live in a city or town that doesn't align with your mindset, maybe you need to make a change. Let's say the culture where you work and reside says, "Forget relationships; forget being in the moment. You need to work your rosy red butt off, have the biggest house, drive the most expensive car, and hang with all the beautiful people." But you're exhausted by constantly pursuing money and status symbols. What you really want is to live a simpler life that enables you to slow down, prioritize your health, and spend time nurturing your relationships. In this case, my friend, you might need to reconsider your zip code.

If relocating isn't in the cards right now (or if you're not sure whether location is actually the root of your unhappiness), you don't have to move to a new city or state. Just go away for the weekend or take a hike (literally) instead of vegging out on your couch. Even a temporary change of scenery and routine can help you look at your boxed-in life with fresh eyes. (And by fresh eyes, I mean having a lightbulb moment where you think, *Wow, I didn't realize how much my life sucked!*) This might be exactly the kick in the pants you need to SNAP.

Expect pushback. This might be the most important piece of advice I share in this chapter. After all, pushback is what causes many people to stay in the box. They aren't prepared to handle criticism and rejection, so they rush back to safety rather than face opposition head-on.

The Proliferation of Pushback

You absolutely have to understand: Pushback is inevitable, because everyone has a damn opinion! We love to stand behind a cause today, and criticism has become a spectator sport. People sometimes seem more defined by what they don't like than by what they support. Just look at social media. If you make a strong statement, you'll immediately attract one group that staunchly defends you and another (probably larger and more vocal) group that violently opposes you.

And let's be honest: You don't even need to log onto Facebook to find people who disagree with just about every life decision you make and every opinion you express. You have relatives, so-called "friends," and competitive coworkers for that, am I right?

Fortunately, forewarned is, to some extent, forearmed. You are more likely to be derailed by opposition when it blindsides you. Here are a few ways to protect yourself:

Anticipate what others are likely to say and compose a response beforehand. Having this sound bite ready to go will help boost your confidence. Plus, hearing you reasonably and rationally explain your decision may prompt people to back off. Of course, you may also need a few zingier comebacks at the ready, like, "Thanks, but when I want your opinion I will give it to you." I also find that a bland expression paired with, "You don't say," works well. (If you really want to beef up your "zinger" arsenal, you can find many more of them in my first book, *Wisdom Wedgies and Life's Little Zingers*, available on Amazon.)

Keep your goal in front of you. I mean that literally. Read through your action plan to remind yourself that building the future you want is worth the pain of pushback.

Ask your accountability team for encouragement and support. You don't have to—and you shouldn't—grapple with rejection and ridicule on your own when there are people in your corner who also believe in your vision.

Remind yourself that someone else's opinion is just that—their opinion. Another person's thoughts and opinions aren't gospel, and they don't have to dictate where you go from here. I once read a photo caption by Meryl Streep that encapsulates this notion beautifully:

"This was me on my way home from an audition for *King Kong* where I was told I was too 'ugly' for the part. This was a pivotal moment for me. This one rogue opinion could derail my dreams of becoming an actress or force me to pull myself up by the boot straps and believe in myself. I took a deep breath and said, 'I'm sorry you think I'm too ugly for your film but you're just one opinion in a sea of thousands and I'm off to find a kinder tide.'"[1]

Given the impressive résumé Meryl has amassed since then, I think we all know how accurate that producer's opinion was!

Designate a detox activity and indulge in it whenever you need to shake off all of the negativity. Brew a cup of tea and read an uplifting book, go to a comedy club, walk your dog, go for a run, meditate or pray, or sweat it out with a punching bag (preferably not your spouse).

Remember that it gets easier with practice. Not everyone in my audiences loves my presentations (shocking, right?!?), and some of them aren't shy about telling me what they disliked and why I'm not their cup of tea. The first few (maybe more than a few) times this happened, I was absolutely crushed. I wondered, *Are they right? Is there something about myself that I can't see? Am I just making a fool out of myself?* I would worry about negative feedback for days, and yes, there were times when

I questioned whether I should just crawl back into my box and never go onstage again.

Fortunately, I have a great team of supporters (especially my mom and my bestie, Kelly), and I didn't quit. It's still not comfortable to hear criticism about my presentations, but over time, it has gotten much easier to focus on the future and refrain from dwelling on negative feedback. I realize that I'll never please everyone, and I don't want to give a relatively small group of naysayers power over my feelings and my future.

Look: Criticism sucks, and I understand why you wouldn't want to subject yourself to it any more than you absolutely have to. Even when it comes from a loving place, it's hard to hear. It feels personal because it *is* personal. But the choice is yours. You can either let it crush you and push you down, or you can push through it and develop better coping skills for next time. The bigger your balls of courage become, the less you'll be bothered by what people who don't support your vision have to say.

Look for nuggets of truth. It pains me somewhat to say it, but sometimes there's a point to other people's opinions. If someone's rejection or criticism is accompanied by a *why*, you should consider whether it has any validity. Maybe you *do* need more experience before taking your career to the next level. Maybe you *should* think about taking on a partner. Maybe this *will* be more expensive than you assumed. Just because you don't like hearing something doesn't automatically make it invalid. Don't throw away an opportunity to learn or improve.

A Whole New Ballgame: Big Balls in Action

Once you've started growing your big balls of courage, they'll help you See and say yes to New Achievable Possibilities—even if some of those possibilities surprise and scare the hell out of you! I'd like to end this chapter by sharing a story about how making a conscious choice to be courageous helped my uncle Bobby Murcer navigate a life-changing offer.

In June 1983, Uncle Bobby got a phone call from Yankees owner George Steinbrenner. Mr. Steinbrenner was already thinking about that year's pennant race, and to give the Yankees their best shot, he wanted Bobby to retire from baseball *that night* to make way for an up-and-coming first baseman named Don Mattingly. Instead of heading onto the field, Bobby would go directly up to the broadcast booth, where Mr. Steinbrenner thought Bobby would continue to be an asset to the franchise. Oh, and if this decision weren't daunting enough, Mr. Steinbrenner needed an answer in 30 minutes![2]

How do you leave a position you love and step into a world you know nothing about? How do you know if you will be a success or a complete failure? How do you know if you are making the biggest mistake of your life? You don't. But sometimes you just have to grow a pair and jump.

That night, Bobby Murcer saw the promise in George Steinbrenner's proposal. And even though it radically changed the future he had previously envisioned for himself, he courageously stepped into the unknown. Of course, in hindsight we all know that Bobby's decision led directly to another amazing 25-year career as a sportscaster.

Here's the bottom line: You've got to have courage—big balls of it—to be happy and to successfully maneuver all the twists and turns life will bring you. And I have yet to meet anyone who was born with big balls of courage. This is an asset you must develop through hard work, perseverance, and pain. But from where I stand, saying yes to new possibilities makes the crazy ride we call life worth it.

So what are you waiting for? The sooner you push through the pain, the sooner you'll reach the passionate life that's waiting on the other side. Can I get a SNAP Yes?!?

Endnotes

1   Alexander, Harriett. "Meryl Streep told she was 'too ugly' to act in King Kong." *The Telegraph*, November 11, 2015. Accessed February 23, 2016. http://www.telegraph.co.uk/news/worldnews/northamerica/usa/11988870/Meryl-Streep-told-she-was-too-ugly-to-act-in-King-Kong.html.

2   Murcer, Bobby. *Yankee for Life: My 40-Year Journey in Pinstripes.* New York: HarperCollins, 2008. 144.

"...IT IS TRUE, EVEN PEOPLE WITH PAINFUL CHILDHOODS...
GROW UP TO BE MORE INTERESTING PEOPLE. SO, THERE'S
ALWAYS A POSITIVE TO A NEGATIVE."
—BARBRA STREISAND

CHAPTER 10

Expect Discomfort. In Fact, Welcome It.

We're all adults here, which means we're all aware that growth and positive change rarely occur without sacrifice and pain. If you want to lose weight and get fit, for instance, you're going to have to sweat it out and say no to unhealthy treats. If you want to transform your backyard into a beautiful garden, you'll have to spend your weekends doing a lot of digging, raking, and heavy lifting. If you want to have a baby, you'll have to deal with sleepless nights, dirty diapers, and disrupted routines (and, if you're a woman, pregnancy and childbirth!).

My point is, struggle and discomfort seem to be part of the human condition—so we might as well accept it and move forward. That advice *definitely* applies to busting out of your box.

It's Time to Look Inward.

In the previous chapter, we talked about things you can do to start moving forward with the SNAP process—the externals, if you will. Here, we'll focus on internals: what you're likely to feel as you grow big balls of courage and how to control those feelings so that they don't control you.

Drop-kicking your box usually involves stubbing your toe. As long as you are taking risks, challenging yourself, and pursuing new goals, discomfort will be your constant companion. As I wrote in the previous chapter, big balls of courage—and the authentic, SNAP-tastic life they enable you to live—are developed only through hard work, perseverance, and pain. As soon as you *stop* feeling uncertainty, fear, doubt, stress, and pushback, you'll know you're in danger of climbing back into your box (or at least bargaining with it).

That said, I believe with every fiber of my being that SNAP-ing is worth the sacrifice, so I want to prepare you for some of the discomfort you're likely to encounter. Here are some common ways in which you can expect SNAP-ing to be, well, less-than-comfy:

You'll have to deal with unpleasant feelings as you face the unknown. Life outside your box is unexplored, unknown territory. (Here be dragons, as the old maps used to say!) It's totally normal to feel anxious, unstable, and maybe even angry about leaving your comfort zone. I have yet to see anyone—whether they're an actor, a professional athlete, a CEO, a stay-at-home mom, or an alligator wrestler—do something they've *never* done before without experiencing an internal vibration we humans label as uncomfortable.

Here's the important distinction you need to make: "Uncomfortable" does not equal "bad." It can, and often does, indicate mental, emotional, physical, and professional growth. As long as you subscribe to the belief that discomfort is negative, you'll go to great lengths to avoid it—and you'll find it very difficult to move far from your box.

You'll have to exert yourself physically. Face it: People are inherently complacent. Saving our energy is the driving force behind so many of humanity's advances and inventions, from the lever and the wheel to television remote controls and robotic vacuum cleaners. And we probably wouldn't be facing an obesity epidemic if people were more willing to get off the couch and go to the gym (or even take the stairs instead of the elevator!).

How does this apply to you? It's simple: Complacent people don't SNAP. You can't just think your way out of a box and into the satisfying life you want. You have to take actual, physical action steps forward. To name just a few possibilities, this might involve getting up early to exercise, traveling to visit a mentor, taking a class, moving to a new city, or putting in extra hours on a work project that's near to your heart.

What Do Woodworking and the OR Have in Common?

You first "met" neurosurgeon Dr. Giancarlo Barolat in Chapter 7, where he wrote about how he has integrated passion into his chosen career. Here, he describes an unexpected physical task he undertook to get to where he is today.

"Growing up in Italy, I always lived in condos and was never required to perform any manual tasks like seasonal upkeep, household repairs, or yard work (unlike what commonly happens when growing up in a house in the USA). I did not have any hobbies that required manual skills. And when I was a resident in neurosurgery at the University of Torino, Italy, I was seldom requested to demonstrate manual skills. As residents, we were not allowed to operate. The 'professor' did all the surgeries, and we were lucky if we could occasionally assist. I finished my five-year residency in neurosurgery having performed, by myself, only two or three very simple operations. (Of course, that contrasts sharply with my second neurosurgical residency, undertaken in the USA, where I performed at least 1,000 surgical procedures on my own!)

"When I first moved to the USA and undertook a one-year specialized program in neurosurgery, I was immediately asked to take a very active role in performing surgical procedures. And this is where I started to fail. I realized that I had never developed the manual skills necessary to be a good surgeon. I was very klutzy in the operating room, and my supervising neurosurgeon picked up on that immediately. Rather than bashing me, he gave me a very useful suggestion. 'You are good,' he said. 'You just have not developed the necessary manual skills. That's what you have to work on for the next six months.' He suggested that I attend woodworking school and use my hands in a constructive way as much as possible.

"For the ensuing eight months, three to four nights a week, after an exhausting day in the operating room, I *did* attend woodworking classes. I made all kind of objects: cabinets, drawers, and wood boxes, to name a few. I became familiar with tools I had never envisioned using. And to my surprise, some of that work was actually applicable to operating on the skull or the spine. Bones are similar, at least in consistency, to wood. And some instruments, including drills, screwdrivers, and saws, are utilized extensively to open the skull and the spine. Through this repetitive almost-daily woodwork, I brought out skills that were dormant in me. Today, almost 40 years later, I truly enjoy performing surgical procedures and have developed a reputation that draws patients from all over the country. Thank you, woodworking! I am so grateful to you!"

Can you imagine how exhausting it would be to attend woodworking class after a long, grueling day working at a hospital? Most of us would want nothing more than to go home and rest, and I'm sure Dr. Barolat felt that way too. But his vision of becoming a skilled neurosurgeon trumped the physical discomfort he felt as he trained his hands to become more dexterous.

The physical sacrifices you're required to make as you SNAP may not be as time- and energy-consuming as those Dr. Barolat committed to—or perhaps they will. Either way, remember that this discomfort is serving a purpose: helping to move you one step closer to the passionate life you want.

You'll have to change your spending habits. Doing something you've never done before might require you to hire a coach or consultant, sign up for training courses, save money to cover a future investment you know is coming, or something similar. SNAP-ing might also mean that you have to take a pay cut or move to a more expensive area of the country. Very rarely does stepping outside the box leave your wallet entirely alone!

Take me, for example. Just because I wanted to be a speaker, and just because I had the ability to stand in front of an audience and engage them, didn't mean that I had all of the training, resources, and expertise I needed to build a successful speaking business. It didn't mean I had the reach or the means to effortlessly attract clients and audiences. I had to set aside money to learn and acquire all of those things. Worth it, *for sure*—but still, there was a fair amount of discomfort involved in stepping away from the budget that I had previously felt safe with. Getting out of the box is freeing, but it isn't cheap.

(One caveat: I'm sure you know this, but "look before you leap" definitely applies here. Make sure you have a solid plan in place before making any major money changes. Dire financial straits can derail everything you've worked for!)

Your relationships with others will change. Anytime you change yourself, the relationships you have with others will change. Sometimes these changes are positive for everyone involved. But it's a sad fact of life that this isn't always the case. People say things like this all the time: *I* *want to see you succeed. I want what's best for you. I'll support you in whatever will make you happy.* But do they *really* mean it?

When I stopped partaking in happy hour (and every other hour), I *expected* to lose my drinking buddies—after all, I knew I'd have to stop spending time with them if I wanted to stay sober. However, I *didn't* expect to lose other longtime friends and even relationships with family members. I would have thought that these people would be my biggest cheerleaders, but instead I found myself ignored, forgotten, gossiped about, and disinvited to the party!

When push comes to shove, many people in your life—your boss, your coworkers, your friends, even your family—won't like how *your* development affects *them*. Your coworkers might not like the redistribution of work that occurs when you take on new projects, for example. Your spouse might not enjoy taking on extra household responsibilities so that you can attend evening classes. Your friends might think that the new, focused you is "no fun." All of these situations might cause grumbling, complaining, snide comments, and wishes for everything to return to "normal."

Other times, people in your life might express doubts because they're genuinely concerned about your welfare. *What if he doesn't succeed? What if she's rejected?* They want to protect you from any pain or disappointment you might experience.

And, as I've mentioned elsewhere, there's the jealousy factor. Many of your boxmates don't really want you to jump out because then they'd have to consider jumping, too. If you want to become an entrepreneur, for instance, your corporate connections might not like hearing you talk about your motivations and plans—because chances are, they're also tired of playing by the rules you're about to leave behind (but they don't have the big balls of courage to do so!). If you initiate a divorce, your bravery in leaving an unsatisfying marriage may threaten friendships with people who wish they weren't too afraid to do the same thing.

Here's the bottom line: If you decide to leave the box, know that you'll be leaving behind some of your lifelong boxmates. It's inevitable—but necessary.

The process of moving forward will force you to relive old pain and heartache. We've already talked about the pain of regret and how much it can affect your happiness and forward progress. Even if you've worked through your old regrets with the *Stop It, Lose It, Use It* process, many of these feelings will bubble up yet again as you see and achieve new possibilities. *Why didn't I do this sooner? How much heartache could I have avoided? I can't believe I let myself be this miserable for this long. I could have prevented so many negative things if I'd acted sooner.*

All of these thoughts are normal—and when you have them, I'd like to refer you back to the *Use It* step. As we've discussed, squelching your pain, fear, and regret won't make these feelings go away—but you *can* use them to fuel positive future change.

Get Comfortable with Discomfort. (Yes, It's Possible!)

Based on my own experiences, I think the initial discomfort you feel right after you SNAP is the worst—though you'll have to deal with it on and off for the rest of your life. The good news is, the more you begin to operate outside of your comfort zone, the more tools you'll acquire to move past fear and stress…and the bigger your big balls of courage will grow.

Here are some of my favorite ways to deal with all of that discomfort we've discussed:

Stop thinking no one else feels this way. From the outside looking in, it may seem like other people don't have any difficulties pursuing their goals. It's all too easy to conclude that you're the only one who seems to be encountering as many setbacks as successes. But the truth is, you're exposed to a very carefully edited version of other people's lives.

Think about it: You'll rarely hear someone sharing at the water cooler that they were turned down for a small business loan. Most people don't detail their struggles with quitting an addiction on Facebook. But that doesn't mean these things aren't happening!

Whether you realize it or not, EVERYONE feels this way when they make big changes in their lives. Once again, discomfort is a universal reaction when stepping into the unknown and confronting your fears. Take comfort in the fact that you're part of a global group of people who have said SNAP Yes! in spite of their own and others' misgivings.

You're in Illustrious Company.

To inspire and motivate you, here are some noteworthy individuals who *definitely* had to deal with a lot of discomfort on the way to achieving success. Fortunately for all of us, they kept their focus on their goals, refused to return to the box, and changed our world. Thanks to Rachel Sugar, Richard Feloni, and Ashley Lutz of *Business Insider* for providing this list.[1] I've excerpted my favorite parts.

- Walt Disney was fired from the *Kansas City Star* because his editor felt he "lacked imagination and had no good ideas."
- Oprah Winfrey was publicly fired from her first television job as an anchor in Baltimore for getting "too emotionally invested in her stories."

- Colonel Harland David Sanders was fired from dozens of jobs before founding a fried chicken empire.
- When Sidney Poitier first auditioned for the American Negro Theatre, he flubbed his lines and spoke in a heavy Caribbean accent, which made the director angrily tell him to stop wasting his time and go get a job as a dishwasher.
- Theodor Seuss Geisel, better known as Dr. Seuss, had his first book rejected by 27 different publishers.
- While developing his vacuum, Sir James Dyson went through 5,126 failed prototypes and his savings over 15 years. But the 5,127th prototype worked, and the Dyson brand became the best-selling bagless vacuum brand in the United States.

Remember that nothing lasts forever. It was inevitable that your favorite TV show would air its final episode sooner or later. Acid-washed jeans and permed hair had their day, and that day is done. The dinosaurs no longer rule the earth. Neither does the Roman Empire. Pluto even lost its place as a full-fledged planet! My point is, all things come to an end eventually—and that includes the discomfort you're feeling right now.

Whenever you're tempted to consider backing off, slowing down, or throwing in the towel entirely, I encourage you to think back on one of your previous "big" accomplishments. How did you feel when you were pulling all-nighters to pass that one incomprehensible class you needed for your degree? When you moved halfway across the country for a new job? When you were asked to lead a project that the entire team's jobs hinged on? When you were in the throes of surviving your kid's terrible twos?

All of those things caused their fair share of anxiety, stress, pain, and exhaustion. But all of that discomfort is in the past now, right? And it was worthwhile, correct? SNAP Yes! Always remember that the fear you feel right now is temporary. Use your present discomfort to motivate you to keep moving forward. As you become more familiar with this new space, the less afraid of it you will be.

Quit telling yourself scary stories. Consider this scenario: You're at work and your boss walks in. He doesn't smile, doesn't say hello, and doesn't act like his normal friendly self. Almost immediately you go into panic mode, wondering if you've done something wrong. You start scanning your memory banks. *Have I been too vocal about sharing my ideas for how our department can improve? Have my evening certification classes been taking more of a toll on my work than I realize? Was the woman who came into the office yesterday applying for my job?* Your stomach goes into knots. You start imagining being out of work, losing your house, being laughed at by your uppity friends, and having to ask your parents for a loan. But guess what? In reality, the only thing "wrong" was that your boss was bloated and constipated!

Yeah, it's easy to laugh at this scenario. But the truth is, we do this kind of thing to ourselves all the time! We decide for ourselves what other people "must" be thinking and why they're "definitely" behaving a certain way. We make decisions and take actions based on what we're afraid *might* happen in the future. We also allow our interpretation of the past (which may or may not be accurate) to determine our current outlooks and attitudes. We torture ourselves by reliving past mistakes and regrets.

What I'm saying is, the stories we tell ourselves are very powerful. Almost singlehandedly, your thoughts have the ability to make an action step feel empowering or burdensome. They have the power to make others' reactions seem crippling or easy to take in stride. They make new possibilities seem achievable or like long shots.

Expert Survey Says: Your Discomfort Might All Be in Your Head.

Dr. Giancarlo Barolat says he can almost always tell which patients are going to suffer the most. No, it's not necessarily the individuals whose conditions are the most serious, or even who are in the most physical pain. It's the people who tell themselves the most negative stories about what they have missed out on, what they're not going to be able to do in the future, and what a bad hand life has dealt them.

Similarly, my late mentor Morty Lefkoe taught that events themselves have no inherent meaning. (In other words, two people might observe or experience the same thing and interpret it in opposite ways.) We assign meaning to the things we see, hear, and experience— and often, the meaning we give these events is incorrect, thus causing us pain and suffering.

So take some time to reflect. How do you think about the physical, financial, and social sacrifices you're making in order to build your best life? Do you see yourself as a victim or as a capable champion? Do you focus on your past failures and mistakes, or do you set your sights on what you'll be able to accomplish in the future? Do you believe there are a limited number of opportunities in the world, or that there's plenty of room for everyone to succeed? Is the discomfort you're currently feeling *really* a necessary consequence of SNAP-ing? Or might some of that pressure and stress be "all in your head"? Can you let any of it go?

Remind yourself that, SNAP Yes!, you're prepared. I have been in front of people speaking, singing, and performing for most of my life. But every single time I hit the stage, I still feel anxiety and butterflies. Does this mean I'm not prepared? NO! Feeling uncomfortable doesn't mean that I'm going to forget my speech or my lines. It just means that I'm getting ready to step in front of an audience I have never encountered before. When I remind myself how many hours I've spent in rehearsal and that I've never fallen off the stage, I'm able to take a deep breath and let the butterflies carry me forward as I step into the spotlight.

As I've said, anytime we step into the unknown, the unfamiliar, or something brand new, we are going to experience uncomfortable internal vibrations. When you find yourself getting stage fright, remind yourself that you didn't get here by accident—you worked hard to create the opportunity in front of you. Think back through the classes you've taken, the conversations you've had with your mentor, the early-morning runs you've put in, or the business plan you've painstakingly revised. Mentally walk yourself through all the action steps you've taken. Then, allow those preparations to give you the courage to keep stepping forward into the brave new world outside your box.

Reconnect with your *why*. Why are you here? Why is it so darn important that you bust out of your box? This is for you to decide—not for me, your parents, or your boss. Your *why* can be answered only for you, by you. (But I do know this: When you define your *why*, *how* to accomplish it will become clearer!) Common *whys* include:

- I want to live my life with more passion.
- I want to stop engaging in behaviors and attitudes that are depressing me, scaring me, and crippling my life.
- It's time to kick my addiction and stop numbing out once and for all.
- I want to prove to myself and others that I'm more than my current job title.
- I want to develop richer relationships with my family and friends.
- I want to build a legacy I'll be proud of at the end of my life.

Basically, your *why* is your emotional fuel for moving forward. Close your eyes for a moment and immerse yourself in your reason(s) for SNAP-ing. This simple exercise can often override any discomfort you're feeling—or at least help you put it in perspective—when you're busy, tired, nervous, or fed up.

Let others help you when the going gets tough. After my uncle retired from playing baseball and went up to the broadcast booth, he decided to take on a big challenge and run the 1988 New York City Marathon. Sometimes we don't realize we miss something until it's gone. Uncle Bobby missed the competitive pace and spirit that professional athletes thrive on, even though he'd hated running during his major league career. So he signed up for the race and trained and trained and trained. Curt Gowdy, Jr., from ABC News even wanted to do a story on him about first-time runners!

The ABC story never came to fruition because of a meeting time mix-up, but it was just as well because at mile 22 Bobby doubled over in a total body cramp. He was forced to move off the course and lie down on the side of the road. Fortunately, his running buddies knew what was happening. They helped him complete those final 4.2-plus miles as he jogged a little, then lay down, jogged a little more, then rested again.

Although his time of 5:00:20 wasn't what Bobby had initially hoped for, he still accomplished his goal of finishing the New York City Marathon.[2] He might never have crossed that finish line at all had it not been for the support of his friends, who sacrificed their own (potential) best times, too.

In this story, Uncle Bobby was dealing mainly with physical discomfort. Your story might involve more mental, emotional, financial, or spiritual discomfort. But whatever the details may be, remember that your friends, family, and coworkers can make the difference between reaching your goals and stopping practically within sight of the finish line. If they're willing, allow them to help you stay the course and share your load. (Return the favor if and when the opportunity arises!) Doubt, fear, stress, and even physical pain don't seem as bad when other people have your back.

Ultimately, here's how I see it: One way or another, you're *always* going to feel uncomfortable. You can choose the discomfort of living in your stressful, limiting, boring box. (Which, as we've already established, just plain sucks.) Or you can choose the discomfort that comes from seeking out new opportunities, experiences, and growth. I hope you always choose to say SNAP Yes! to option number two, because that's the path to lifelong fulfillment, engagement, and improvement.

Endnotes

1   Sugar, Rachel, Richard Feloni, and Ashley Lutz. "29 famous people who failed before they succeeded." *Business Insider*, July 9, 2015. Accessed February 8, 2016. http://uk.businessinsider.com/successful-people-who-failed-at-first-2015-7?r=US&IR=T.

2   Murcer, Bobby. *Yankee for Life: My 40-Year Journey in Pinstripes.* New York: HarperCollins, 2008. 222-23.

"I'M SCARED OF AUDIENCES."
—ADELE

CHAPTER 11

If It Scares You, Say SNAP Yes! to It

Remember my first experience with skydiving? I was so petrified that I was honestly afraid I'd pee myself when it was my turn to get sucked out into the wild blue yonder. You probably also recall that I ended up *loving* skydiving (and did not need a change of pants afterward). Free-falling through the air gave me the most wonderful sense of boundlessness and exhilaration.

Of course, that's also what it's like to SNAP. The most intimidating step forward is often the one that pays off the most, because it takes you farthest from your box.

So here's my question: What scares the pee out of you? What do you *know* you need to do, but are avoiding because it seems too difficult or uncomfortable or daunting? What scary thing are you avoiding saying SNAP Yes! to?

What I DON'T Mean by "Scary"

To make sure we're on the same page upfront, let me explain what I *don't* mean by "doing what scares you."

"Scary" looks different for everyone. You know how you can laugh through a horror movie while your friend cringes behind a throw pillow? (Or maybe it's the other way around!) That's also true when it comes to SNAP-ing. What one person finds frightening might not cause another to bat an eyelash.

So when I talk about "scary stuff," I'm not referring to what's scary for your friend or colleague or brother. You don't accomplish anything meaningful by proving that you can do what someone else can't or won't. I'm talking about what's scary for *you*. The idea is to tackle something that *you* find incredibly intimidating. Which brings me to my next point…

SNAP-ing isn't *Fear Factor*. I'm not encouraging you to do something *just because* it's scary. "Frightening" and "wise" are not always synonymous. (As far as I know, the only place where you get a paycheck just for doing something terrifying is on reality TV.) Sometimes, fear serves the very important purpose of telling you to STOP IT, STOP IT, STOP IT! You must always assess the risks associated with saying yes before you take a big leap away from your box.

So please, don't tell your boss to "take this job and shove it" if you don't know where your next paycheck will come from. Don't agree to go mountain climbing if you don't know a carabiner from a crampon. Don't say yes to having kids if you really don't want them. Don't take on a larger mortgage and figure out how to pay for it later. *Uh, uh—no way!* Risk management isn't negotiable, people!

Risk Management at Work

Most people find SNAP-ing at work to be especially challenging. One of the (many!) reasons is that we have so much to lose if we screw up. (You know—things like our paychecks, insurance, homes, and credibility...no biggie!) When confronted by these high stakes, it's very easy for fear to get the best of us and keep us in the box.

I asked Linda Rutherford to share her thoughts on how we can manage fear and risk while still saying SNAP Yes! at work. As the vice president and chief communications officer of Southwest Airlines, Linda has a lot of experience in this area—and a lot of wisdom to share. Here's what she has to say:

"In our professional lives, we are immersed in risk, risk management, risk aversion, and risk taking. It can all be overwhelming and in some cases paralyzing. I've noticed that as we grow in our careers, we are prone to take fewer and fewer risks because the stakes seem higher and failure can happen on a much grander stage. Here are some tactics to help you climb the success ladder while still taking intelligent risks—not to mention a deep breath every now and then.

- **Be a committed student of your company.** You have to know your organization well enough to understand the formal and informal power structures, where the sensitivities are, and what methods for debate and dialogue are most productive. Be an observer, take note of nonverbal communication in meetings, and watch for patterns that can help you make wise decisions in the future.

- **Remind yourself that you didn't get this far by accident.** If you have been identified for a position in leadership, it's not just because you are good at what you do functionally—there are plenty of good accountants, strategists, analysts, etc. Someone saw in you the ability to quickly or intuitively slice through a delicate issue with ease; or they saw an ability to motivate and inspire others that not everyone possesses; or you have a needed and appreciated perspective. So even if the next step feels risky or scary, remember that you're moving forward from a proven foundation of success.

- **Embrace that your perspective is crucial.** You have to share it. Yes, that might mean taking a risk and sharing an unpopular stance. HOW you choose to share it is key; I learned that lesson once when I was asked for my thoughts on a particularly sensitive issue. I took the request at face value and blurted out my opinions and perspective. It backfired—not because of *what* I shared, but because of *how* I chose to do it in a room full of people. I learned to take stock of the audience, stall if I needed to in order to provide the information in a better venue, be thoughtful about who should receive the message, and carefully consider how to share it (verbal, written, etc.).

"I've seen good leaders muted because they didn't want to take the personal risk of speaking up or stepping up. You have to push beyond that and find productive ways to share your perspective, knowledge, and strengths."

What I DO Mean by "Scary"

Now that we've gotten my disclaimers out of the way, what *do* I consider "good" things to say SNAP Yes! to...in spite of the fact that they may scare you to death? As we discussed earlier in this book, just about every step you take away from your box will be frightening (or at least uncomfortable). However, I'm guessing there are one or two things that overshadow the others. This is the action step you've been avoiding as you tackle everything else on your to-do list, or maybe the one you're (unsuccessfully) trying to convince yourself isn't necessary.

Here are some examples of action steps that have scared the crap out of people I know:

- Speaking in front of a crowd in order to present research at a professional conference
- Volunteering to lead an exploratory task force to identify new markets this person's company might be able to break into

- Firmly disagreeing with a respected authority figure who believed this person should find a "new" or "different" goal
- Confronting a bullying client
- Making (informed, well-researched!) changes to a budget in order to pay for schooling
- Cutting ties with unhealthy "friends" who had been in this person's life for years
- Deciding to grow a "personal" philanthropy into a nonprofit
- Ending an unhealthy, abusive marriage and taking self-defense classes

Personally, when I first stepped onto the speaking stage, I knew I wanted singing to be a part of my talk. But did I *really* want to put myself out there as a performer? Here I was in my late forties, launching my career at a time when most singers are thinking about retiring their chops. What if people thought performing during a motivational speech was silly, or hated my voice, or worse, said I sucked? Public speaking was easy, but delivering words set to a tune? That was a super gamble, and just the thought of it made my mouth go dry.

But here's what I know: When you put yourself out there authentically, it touches people in an unexpected and personal way. I believe that singing is one of the things (perhaps THE thing!) that differentiates me as a speaker and has helped me build a successful career. What I also know is that my talent was always there. The only thing that got in the way of my using it were the limiting beliefs in my head.

Are Scary Steps Worth It?

You might be asking yourself, *How do I know for sure that doing what scares me will be worth it? What if the positive impact on my life is minimal, while the stress of moving forward is overwhelming?*

There are exceptions to every rule, of course, but this generally isn't the case. If you've done the work of closely examining your box and setting SNAP-tastic goals accordingly, you'll be able to tell when the benefits of a scary step are likely to outweigh the costs. Furthermore, when you've done your risk-management due diligence, the payoff you get tends to equal—or outweigh!—the amount of fear you overcame.

So yes—scary steps *are* worth it. But don't just take my word for it. Here are the stories of two people I know who transformed their lives because they had the courage to say SNAP Yes! in spite of fear.

Kari Warberg Block is the founder and CEO of Earth-Kind, which manufactures pest prevention products, rodent repellent, and air fresheners—all of which are all-natural, toxin-free, and safe for the environment. She's also passionate about coaching and supporting small businesses and entrepreneurs. Here's her story, in her own words:

"Opportunity is often disguised in pain and suffering. In my case, I was about to lose my mind because of rodent damage on my family's New Town, North Dakota, farm. Those wild mice got into everything: our tractors (causing thousands of dollars of damage), my greenhouse (where they ate stock that had already been sold), and my daughter's tack room (contaminating horse feed that didn't exactly come cheap). In short, my unwelcome rodent guests were painfully expensive, and to complicate matters, there wasn't a safe way to deal with the problem.

"So, I thought, *If it's going to be, it's going to have to come from me!* I ended up inventing the first plant-based rodent repellent to meet federal EPA standards for professional use. The product that came to be known as Fresh Cab® is a thoughtfully designed sachet that repels by aroma, reliably keeping mice out of any area where it's been placed for up to three months. It's safe to use around kids and pets too!

"Over the next several years, I tried to license my invention, but no one was interested. So I took a big scary leap into the unknown and commercialized it myself. To help put into perspective just how daunting this decision was, I not only had no experience in the pest control industry; I also had no money and didn't even own a computer! I was facing the very real possibility that if my venture didn't succeed, I'd lose everything.

"But I did have one important thing going for me—something that gave me the courage to say SNAP Yes! in spite of my fear: I was confident that other people would buy my invention. Why? Even though it was more expensive than conventional poisons, it was *safe*. Plus, it's so much easier to keep rodents out altogether than it is to lure them in, only to kill them with poison or traps and then have to clean up their bodies!

"To make a long story short, that first invention is now a $50 million brand! And because of my business's success, I'm able to pursue other passions: I employ the handicapped, travel around the world helping people, and serve as an advisor to Congress, the Small Business Administration, and the White House. It's a life I couldn't have ever imagined if I hadn't taken a leap into the scary unknown.

"My best advice is, when something really pisses you off, it may be a huge opportunity in disguise! So step forward. If you wait too long, you'll likely be late. I acted before 'natural' was popular, and it gave me time to get Fresh Cab® and Stay Away® Rodent into stores across the nation before the big guys even realized humane and natural pest control was an unmet market need."

Betsy Jourdan works as a mortgage loan originator at Pinnacle Bank and (as you'll see!) in the funeral services industry. She wrote the following about how facing one of her biggest fears helped her to establish a meaningful and fulfilling career:

"For most of my life, I was petrified of funerals, funeral homes, and most things associated with the loss of a loved one. At 42 I experienced my first major loss when my very special 'adopted father' took his own life. Five months later, my equally wonderful biological father passed from chronic illness.

"While coping with these losses, a light went off inside of me. Despite my lifelong fear of death and dying, I decided that I wanted to explore a possible career in assisting others with grief...perhaps a career in the funeral services industry? As often seems to happen, life soon offered me the opportunity to say yes to a career in funeral services—one that dealt mainly with family interaction, speaking, and teaching about grief.

"I was afraid (okay, *terrified*) to take this huge leap into the unknown—but also excited. With the help of a great public speaker and lots of friends and family, I moved forward with baby steps. Working a few visitations and funerals were my early adventures in the mortician world. And then, along came the big one. Four months into my new career, my best friend passed suddenly and unexpectedly! I assisted her family from start to finish as they tried to understand, process, and move forward—perhaps the ultimate test for someone working in funeral services.

"I've learned that sometimes, the things we fear most produce and develop the greatest hidden gifts within us. Death freaked me out big time. But once I dug in and learned what it meant, how it affected people (including myself), and how to move on, I was able to tap into work that I'm truly passionate about."

Learn to Walk With Fear

Taking scary steps toward your goals is one of those things that's *definitely* easier said than done. I should know—at various points in my life I've tried to erase anxiety and nerves with hypnosis, alcohol, and praying till I'm blue in the face. Surprise, surprise—none of them worked. My fear was still there at the end of the day. And for several decades, I allowed it to hold me back from taking steps toward a life I didn't need to numb out of.

After I finally SNAP-ed and answered one of the increasingly loud wake-up calls life was sending me, I realized that being scared of risk and growth is something that will never go away—but it *is* something that can be managed.

For example, I'm no stranger to public speaking or performing, but I still feel stage fright every time I'm about to step out in front of an audience. That's true whether I'm speaking to a small group, singing in front of 48,000 people at Yankee Stadium, or keynoting a conference with 5,000 attendees. Here are some of the tactics that keep me saying yes to these opportunities in spite of primal instincts that urge me to run:

Notice how much time it takes you to calm down. I've learned that once I hit the stage it's going to be about three minutes before the anxiety disappears and I begin to feel in my element. This knowledge helps me to accept, live with, and even welcome my fear instead of fighting it.

The next time you're in a stressful or scary situation (assuming it's not unhealthy or dangerous—duh!), pay attention to how long it takes to regain your equilibrium. Better yet, try to keep tabs on your fear in a variety of different circumstances. Once you've learned what to expect from your mind and body, give yourself that amount of time as a grace period the next time you're facing an important decision or thinking of throwing in the towel.

Have a plan to help you move the anxiety out. Just because you know how long your fear is likely to stick around doesn't mean you can't help it on its way out the door! I purposefully design my talks to include a lot of movement (from me, and sometimes even from the audience) in those first few minutes. If you've ever attended one of my keynotes, you may have seen me jump out of a box and dance with the audience.

This helps me move the adrenaline out of my system so that I can focus on the information I want to deliver.

Before you take your own scary step forward, come up with a similar plan. For instance, if you are going to lead a meeting, tell a joke at the beginning to make people laugh, or ask a question to get others talking so you have time to calm down. If you need to have a difficult conversation, practice a few relaxing yoga poses or do some deep breathing beforehand.

Schedule what scares you. When you're excited about something, you'll make sure it happens. (That's why you never miss your golf tee time or forget to watch your favorite TV show, am I right?) But when something stressful or frightening is looming on the horizon, it's all too easy to put it off or forget about it entirely. You know how it is: "I'll call that client tomorrow" turns into "I'll call her next week," which turns into the *next* week, ad infinitum.

Hence my advice to you: The next time you're facing a scary step forward, put it on the calendar. There's something about seeing a concrete deadline that moves us to action. If your task involves other people, all the better. Knowing that they're expecting you to show up or step up will further fuel your motivation to pull a Nike and "just do it." And heck, while you're at it, schedule yourself a nice little reward—like a massage or a night out with friends—once you've accomplished your goal. The carrot works just as well as the stick!

Break it down... When I made the decision to stop drinking, I had to stay focused on one step, one minute, and one day at a time. That's why AA has the 12-step program. (You don't jump from step 1 to step 12 in a SNAP. Skipping all of the important lessons and growth in between would be the quickest path to relapse and failure!) I had to ruthlessly watch my thoughts and not allow my mind to drift too far into the future. Back then, it had been years since I went two days without a drink. The thought of not drinking for the rest of my life would have ignited my anxiety, kindled the belief that "this was impossible," and sent me running right back to my Cabernet Sauvignon box!

You may not be working through a 12-step program. But if the thing that scares you involves numerous phases or steps (like transitioning to a different department at work or moving to a new location), you still need to break it down into bite-sized pieces. Don't worry about step 10—say, getting assigned to a certain project in the new department—if you're stuck on step 4, which is telling your current boss that you want to change trajectories.

...And stay focused on the task at hand. I'm well aware that staying focused on step 4 when you're really worried about step 10 is much easier said than done. So how do you ignore all of the scary what-ifs and worst-case scenarios that keep distracting you from the present moment? Taking a few deep breaths, counting to 10, walking around the block, or watching a funny movie can all be surprisingly effective at helping you refocus on the here and now. Buckling down and checking an item off your to-do list can also boost your confidence and deflate your worries.

But the most effective way to stop being a hostage to future fears is to quit telling yourself stories that haven't even started, much less end in regret (or as my mom always says, "borrowing trouble that isn't there"). In the next chapter, we'll examine how you can tune out the voice in your head that constantly tries to convince you that your limiting beliefs are the gospel truth.

Talk it out. Remember when I advised you to find a mentor or role model to help you grow your big balls of courage? This would be a great time to take advantage of that person's knowledge and experience. Someone who has been there, done that, and bought the t-shirt can quickly talk you down when you get worked up. "I was terrified when I stood in your shoes—but saying yes was one of the best decisions I ever made" can be one of the most comforting, courage-boosting sentences you'll ever hear. "Let me give you some pointers on moving forward" is even better.

Remember your regrets... Reminding yourself of what regret feels like can sometimes be the nudge you need to step forward. Upon serious consideration, you may find that even acute fear does not outweigh the crushing burden of regret. Remember, the boxes we put ourselves in are not biodegradable; they will not fall apart on their own. Would you rather risk seeing some of your fears come true...or guarantee that you'll stay dissatisfied and disengaged?

...And savor your successes. Each time you do say SNAP Yes! in spite of fear, allow yourself to fully experience how great it feels. Take a few moments to congratulate yourself and bask in your accomplishment before moving on to the next task. Recognize how much more confident and excited you are when you end the day feeling successful instead of defeated by procrastination. This sets up the success momentum for the next day, and the next, and the next!

Realize that you'll live if your fears *do* become reality. What's the worst thing that will happen if you take that scary step forward and your fears become a reality? Will you lose a friendship? Your boss's respect? A job opportunity? Your job? Your house? A portion of your savings? It won't be fun, but think through—in detail—exactly how failure will impact your life.

If your worst fears might actually threaten your health or ability to provide life's basic necessities, perhaps you need to take more time to prepare, create a Plan B (and C!), or research alternate paths forward.

In many cases, though, you'll find that even if your worst fears *do* come true, you have the resources to weather the storm, regroup, and rebuild. You'll ultimately be okay. You may even realize that several months or years down the road, the failure you're dreading will barely even register as a blip in your life's radar. In its own way, that knowledge is very reassuring and can give you the confidence to finally step forward.

Ultimately, though, I think Winston Churchill was right. He said, "When I look back on all these worries, I remember the story of the old man who said on his deathbed that he had had a lot of trouble in his life, most of which had never happened."

Finally, resolve to answer when fear unexpectedly knocks on your door. Sometimes you're in full control of whether or not to take a scary step forward. At other times, you may find yourself forced to the edge of the precipice by events that are out of your control.

For instance, maybe your company is downsizing...and you're holding a pink slip. Maybe your boss asks if you'd like to answer the department VP's question during a meeting you had expected to only observe. Maybe your friend pulls you aside at her rehearsal dinner and asks if you'll sing at the wedding because the previous vocalist came down with laryngitis. Maybe you've just received a life-threatening diagnosis and need to make big changes in order to reduce your stress level. Or maybe your investing-savvy spouse has passed away and you're faced with learning how to manage your own finances.

Even in these unexpected situations, you have a choice: take hold of your courage and jump, or climb back into the box.

My colleague Bob Tipton, who is a phenomenal transformational change speaker, found himself in just such a situation as a young businessman. I'll let him share his story in his own words:

"They had that stereotypical government vibe about them: dark suits, white shirts, style-free ties, sensible shoes, and eight-dollar haircuts. Helping to further set the scene was the fact that they brought a chain and padlock with them, as well as a notice that read 'Seized' in red, 120-point font. They were in the process of attaching both to the door of my company when I arrived.

"When I woke up that morning, I thought it was going to be just another normal day as a struggling entrepreneur. I had no idea that I'd encounter a pair of humorless, robotic IRS agents when I came to work.

"I'll fast forward through the 'oh shit' conversation I had with myself, as well as the stammering, pleading, 'I had no idea' vomit of verbiage I threw at both agents. Suffice it to say, my 29-year-old mind was racing, my blood pressure skyrocketed, and I was thrust into a desperate attempt to stave off a death sentence for my business.

"Eventually (after what seemed like hours, but was probably only six or eight minutes), Agents 'Unfriendly' and 'Unfeeling' finally shared with me the basis for their mission that morning. I had a problem—a big problem. It turned out that unbeknownst to me, our 'business administrator' had just been paying net payroll for several months due to cash flow shortages. In other words, the IRS never received the withholding we should have been paying them. The federal government doesn't like it when you mess with withholding taxes. Imagine that!

"My unsophisticated, ignorant, and just plain poor approach to running my business had caught up with me. I'd trusted the wrong people and had abdicated my responsibilities as the owner. I was screwed... or so I thought.

"Then something incredibly simple turned the whole situation around almost immediately. (You might even say in a SNAP!) You see, IRS agents are trained and prepared to encounter belligerent, angry, low-accountability responses when they take their business seizure show on the road. What they're not expecting is vulnerability, authenticity, contrition, and flexibility.

"What 'saved' me was the fact that I wasn't trying to not pay taxes or avoid my responsibility; I was just a blissfully ignorant and (at the time) bad business manager. Despite my screw-up, I was, at heart, a rule-following, high-integrity guy.

"Once I realized what my situation truly entailed, I took my first step forward into the unknown: I stopped trying to convince the agents of anything and accepted the reality that was in front of me. (If you've ever had to raise the white flag of surrender to the IRS, you know just how daunting that can be!) Then I took full responsibility for what had happened and requested, in as selfless a manner as I could muster, some time to work out a 'both-and' solution. Fully expecting to be rejected (and maybe also lectured and escorted off the property), I asked for the opportunity to BOTH keep the doors open AND find a way to make things right with the IRS.

"After a few terse phone calls with their supervisors, some super-secret hallway conversations between themselves, and some scribbling on their low-bidder-manufactured yellow pads, Agents 'Unfriendly' and 'Unfeeling' had a response to my proposal: 'Yes, you may keep operating your business. AND you will agree to a comprehensive audit of all your business operations over the past two years. Plus, you will enter into a binding legal agreement that guarantees repayment of your tax liability through your personal assets.' (Or something like that...this was more than 25 years ago!)

"The next six months were the most challenging of my professional career, but they were also the most educational. I learned (and lived) the difference between *saying* you're committed and *being* committed. As it turned out, those steps I took to stave off the wrath of the IRS were just the beginning. I soon found myself making many more unexpected decisions that felt frightening and risky as I worked on saving my business, managing it responsibly, and becoming fully transparent.

"I might never have taken *any* of those steps—which all turned out to be beneficial—had I not been forced to do so by my buddies Agents 'Unfriendly' and 'Unfeeling.' But because those guys *did* show up with a padlock, I improved my business. I found a new respect for myself when it came to doing the right thing, the right way. Most importantly,

I pulled my head out of my 'I'm a 20-something entrepreneur, and this is FUN!' way of thinking and became genuinely committed to learning what, how, and when to do what was needed.

"By the way—we repaid every cent to the government."

The more often you say SNAP Yes! in spite of your fear, the more often life will give you the opportunity to do so. So be brave…again, and again, and again. No one else can take transformative risks for you—but then again, no one else stands to reap the SNAP-tastic rewards. Can I get a SNAP Yes?!?

"I wish I could be like Shaw who once read a bad review of one of his plays, called the critic, and said: 'I have your review in front of me and soon it will be behind me.'"
—Barbra Streisand

CHAPTER 12

Silence Your Inner Bette Davis

If you were paying attention in Chapter 4, you might remember me talking about my relationship with Bette Davis. (No, not the *real* Bette Davis; a version of her who lived—still lives, actually—in my head.) Let's recap: Sometime in college I began to doubt that I had the ability to achieve my dream of singing on Broadway. And every time my doubts cropped up, they sounded exactly like Bette Davis.

DeDe, dah-ling, you're not a little girl anymore. Isn't it time your dream grew up too? Do you really think you have what it takes to beat out all those other talented people on Broadway? You'll be scraping by, waiting tables, while other people get all the roles you wanted. Wouldn't it be better to do something you know *you'll be a success at, dah-ling? Something that will give you money and power?*

As you know, I listened to Bette. I changed my trajectory and pursued a corporate sales career that *did* bring me money and success. Bette was happy—but I wasn't. It took me over two decades to realize that Bette's opinion was not the gospel truth, and that I didn't have to let my doubts dictate my life.

Who Is Bette, and How the Heck Did She Get in My Head?

Guess what, friends? We *all* have a Bette Davis living inside of our heads. She's your internal critic, the one who voices your doubts, fears, and negative what-ifs. She's the enemy within who interferes with the pursuit of your personal and career goals. She's a big advocate of box bargaining, and she's also really good at causing your big balls of courage to shrink. She's one of the main things that keeps you in your box and lures you back to it once you've SNAP-ed.

Bette Has a Lot of Colleagues.

Your inner critic might not sound like Bette Davis. He or she might sound like Stephen Colbert giving you a hard time, like Donald Trump berating an apprentice, like your eighth grade teacher calling you out in front of the class, or like your mother giving you a stern lecture. To keep things simple, though, I'm going to refer to your inner critic as Bette.

Where does Bette come from? I believe she's the combined voice of all the people who have influenced and impacted you the most: your parents, teachers, coaches, bosses, friends, and significant others. She's likely to remind you the most of authority figures from your childhood.

Think about it: When you were a kid, you believed that certain people in your life *absolutely* knew what was best for you. You trusted what they told you, and you internalized their behaviors and outlooks. Most importantly, you developed the belief that their reactions to you and their fears for you were immutable truths.

Up to the age of seven or so, children think that everything is about them or because of them. *My teacher is angry? I must have been bad or lazy or stupid. My parents are getting a divorce? I should have done something to keep that from happening. My friend called me a mean name? I must have done something wrong.* And throughout their formative years, even after they understand that not everything is about them, children pick up messages from others' facial expressions, tone of voice, body language, words, and more. Unfortunately, these messages are often incorrect and are difficult to override.

For example, when you're seven years old and you get an "Unsatisfactory" on your report card, you don't have the ability to stand back and think, *My mom is yelling because she is stressed, she wants the best for me, and she's worried about my future. Mom feels like she didn't try enough in school and therefore has to work harder today. She loves me so much, and she doesn't want me to have the same regrets she does.* Instead, you think, *I have to be perfect in order for others to approve of me, love me, and not cause me pain. The only way to avoid this in the future is to never make mistakes and keep people satisfied at all times.*

In this example, you might grow up to find that Bette is a perfectionist. *If you aren't sure you can do this right, dah-ling, maybe you should consider something else. After all, nothing is worse than failure! What will people think of you if you trip—or fall flat on your face?* (If your inner critic sounds more like Donald Trump, the message you hear might sound more like, *If you screw this up even a little bit, YOU'RE FIRED!*)

Is Bette Davis Sharing Your Office?

Bette can be particularly destructive in the workplace. Because your professional performance is directly tied to your paycheck (which you depend on to fund the rest of your life), you might be particularly inclined to play it safe when you're on the clock. But when you allow Bette to keep you from asserting yourself, making changes, and taking risks, you're only limiting yourself.

Here are five things Bette might say to hold you back at work—and why I think her professional advice is bogus.

1. **Bette says:** *You'd better not turn in your project or submit your idea until you've ironed out all the kinks. You don't want to give your boss a sloppy piece of crap.*

   DeDe says: There will *always* be modifications and tweaks you can make to your work, because there's no such thing as perfection! Don't let the right opportunity pass you by while you're focused on getting rid of all possible mistakes. In business *and* in life, a great idea that's still in development is much more valuable than a perfect idea that never sees the light of day.

2. **Bette says:** *If you push back or speak up against a strong personality or top leader, you will not be respected. You might even be demoted and fired. So just zip your lips and deal with it!*

   DeDe says: Your superiors are looking for potential leaders, not sycophants and yes-men. Not making waves isn't the way to make it into the corner office (or generally, achieve any of your goals). There's a respectful, constructive way to phrase any alternate opinions you may have.

3. **Bette says:** *As a woman, it's not worth your time to step up in your male-dominated field. All of the pushback you'll encounter just isn't worth it, and you'll constantly have to prove yourself to the members of the good old boys' club. Just keep quiet and be happy with the job you have.*

   DeDe says: What?!? This is the 21st century. The fact that a man has traditionally held the position you want doesn't mean anything. If you are passionate about achieving a professional goal and you know that you have the necessary skills, you owe it to yourself to give it your all. Bette should be ashamed of herself. (By the way, as one of the first women to become really successful as a forklift salesperson, I speak from experience here.)

4. **Bette says:** *You're still not enough. You don't have enough education, enough experience, enough charisma…you just don't have enough.*

   DeDe says: This line of thinking might drive you to get more training and education, but it will never enable you to obtain the position or project you really want! Trust me: When faced with taking a big step outside their comfort zone, *everyone* feels unqualified and inadequate. More than training, experience, education, etc., the one thing that separates SNAP-ers from box dwellers is the conviction that they *can* and *will* do what is necessary to create the future they want.

5. **Bette says:** *You should be thankful for your job. Look at all the layoffs and cutbacks! Don't dwell on your unhappiness, you ungrateful twit!*

   DeDe says: The fact that your current employer or position is providing you with a paycheck does not obligate you to stay there forever. You can be thankful that you are making a living while still working toward other goals.

No matter how long it's been since you SNAP-ed or how far away you've kicked your box, Bette will always be lurking somewhere in your mind, ready to pounce during a moment of doubt or weakness. You see, Bette never says, *Well, dah-ling, my work here is done. I'm completely confident that you know what you're doing. Goodbye!* She's forever hard-wired into our brains, so it's important to learn to deal with her.

The good news is, you can grow your big balls of courage so large and hone your awareness to so precise a point that Bette becomes more like a little gnat buzzing around your head instead of an 800-pound gorilla roaring and pounding his chest. In the rest of this chapter, I'll share some strategies to help you overpower and outsmart Bette's voice.

Recognize That Bette Is There and That She Is Powerful.

Since you can't evict Bette from your brain, it's important to come to an understanding with her. Hating her won't do you any favors, because (like it or not) Bette is a part of you—and self-loathing always leads to self-destruction.

Instead, I suggest learning to respect Bette. Acknowledge that in her own twisted way, she wants the best for you and is trying to protect you. *Thanks, but no thanks, Bette!* Then, really get to know her voice and her tactics so that you'll be able to recognize them when they crop up. Regularly check in with your thoughts, attitudes, and motivations to make sure that they don't sound like Bette.

You can't leave your mind on autopilot, because this is an open invitation for Bette to come in and start taking over. You see, on a basic instinctual level, we *all* want to take the safe, easy path through life, and if you aren't paying attention, Bette will take the wheel and drive full-speed back toward your box.

The Brain Is Hardwired to Enable Bette.

Professor Daniel Kahneman shines a light on this concept in his book *Thinking Fast and Slow*. (Professor Kahneman was awarded a Nobel Prize in economic-science in 2002, so he knows what he's talking about!) Our brains, he writes, are made up of two "systems." The following explanation was summarized by Erik Johnson:

"System 1 fills in ambiguity with automatic guesses and interpretations that fit our stories. It rarely considers other interpretations. When System 1 makes a mistake, System 2 jumps in to slow us down and consider alternative explanations. 'System 1 is gullible and biased to believe, System 2 is in charge of doubting and unbelieving, but System 2 is sometimes busy, and often lazy,' (page 81). "Potential for error? We are prone to over-estimate the probability of unlikely events (irrational fears) and accept uncritically every suggestion (credulity)."[1]

Fortunately, as they say, knowing is half the battle. When you are aware that your brain is hardwired to enable Bette, you'll be less likely to take her at her word. Before making a big decision, pause and double-check that System 2 isn't taking the day off!

Separate the SNAP-tastic Part of Yourself from Bette.

Yes, Bette may be a permanent resident in your brain, but you must learn to look at her in the third person. Give your inner critic a name, a look, a persona, and a voice. As is the case with me, maybe your Bette will resemble a celebrity. Or maybe you'll create a persona from scratch.

It may seem hokey, but I want you to actually get into the habit of thinking, *Bette Davis/John Wayne/Eeyore/Critic McNaysayer is telling me that voicing my concerns to the boss is a terrible idea, and that I should just keep my mouth shut.* That thought has a much different ring to it than this one: *I'm stupid for voicing my concerns.*

The point is to help you see that you do not have to "be" your thoughts. You have the power to See New Achievable Possibilities that Bette has never even considered—and to make them a reality. Plus, it's much easier to say no to Bette than it is to defy yourself. See? Having multiple personalities isn't always a bad thing.

Bust the Beliefs That Bette Is Pushing.

The late Morty Lefkoe was a pioneer in busting limiting beliefs, as well as the founder and CEO of the Lefkoe Institute. According to Morty, you cling to your limiting beliefs because you believe that you actually *saw* your limits at some point in your life (usually, during childhood).[2, 3]

For example, when you think, *I'm not good enough*, you might automatically see a mental image of your parents being critical. It's important to prove to yourself that you never actually *saw* yourself not being good enough; you saw your parents' behavior. Their reaction to you is not an immutable truth about you (regardless of what Bette might have to say about it!).

These are the steps I use to put Morty's teachings into practice:

1. Determine the belief that Bette is using to hold you back; e.g., *I'm not good enough, I'm not smart enough, Mistakes and failures are bad*, etc.

2. Pinpoint when you first remember having this thought. Be as detailed as possible in creating a mental image.

3. List who was there with you. What behaviors on their part led to your belief?

4. List five alternate reasons for their behavior. For example, let's say you believe that you're "not good enough" because your father yelled at you after you got in trouble at school. You specifically remember him saying he wished you were more like your older brother. He might have reacted this way not because he *really* believed you weren't as good as your brother, but because:

   - He'd had a stressful day at work and his frustration spilled over into his interaction with you.
   - He was dreading the difficult conversation that might happen at the next parent/teacher conference.
   - He was afraid other parents would judge his worth as a father based on your behavior.
   - He thought the comparison to your older brother would motivate you.
   - This is how his own parents reacted when he made mistakes.

5. Describe what not being good enough (or whatever your limiting belief is) looks like. When you see something, it has a color, a size, a shape, etc. So what does "not good enough" look like? Can you actually see it in front of you the way you see this book? (If you're drawing a blank, well, that's the point!)

6. Realize that you didn't actually see "I'm not good enough." You assigned a meaning to an event or to someone else's behavior (which isn't accurate because events in and of themselves have no meaning).

7. Understand that you picked up one possible truth and, with Bette's encouragement, have lived as if it is "THE" truth for your entire life. What if you had picked up another truth? What if instead you'd said, "I'm so good and so lovable that my dad wants the absolute best for me"? How would you see risk and failure now?

8. Ask yourself where your interpretation originated. If you didn't see it in reality, where did you see it? The answer: Only in your mind. That's the great news, because if you created that belief, then you can throw it out and pick up another truth. Make it one that will allow you to step up, speak up, and show up as your best self.

9. Finally, don't play the "What if I'm just kidding myself about being a wonderful, capable, and smart person?" game. SNAP out of it! Don't read that story, because you know who's writing it? Bette!

Focus on Your Big Balls of Courage Instead of on Bette.

Remember the strategies I shared in Chapter 9 about how you can grow your big balls of courage in the face of uncertainty and fear? If you focus on them, they'll help guide you away from what Bette is saying...while discrediting her in the process.

Realize That Other People Don't Give a Crap!

When Bette is regaling you with her opinions, it's easy to believe that she's saying what everyone else is thinking. But guess what? You're giving Bette so much more credit than she deserves. Trust me—nine and a half times out of ten, you are definitely your own worst critic. Most of the people whose opinions you value the most want you to succeed. If you could read their minds, their thoughts about you would sound nothing like Bette's.

(Of course, there will always be naysayers who inevitably butt in with their negative opinions—we've discussed them and how to handle their pushback in previous chapters.)

But *most* people—the ones who never bother to voice a positive *or* negative opinion about your life? They simply don't care! They're too consumed with their own lives to concentrate on yours. They don't give a crap about whether you're smart enough, have the necessary skills, or are doomed to failure. Besides, if people want to be entertained by someone else's problems, they can obsess about the Kardashians or the Real Housewives of Wherever from the comfort of their couches. As long as you can keep your efforts and challenges off of reality TV, social media, and the evening news, rest assured that the world is not spending its time judging you. Isn't that a relief?

One of my friends—I'll call her Denise—was recently invited to a Zumba class. "Oh no, I don't do Zumba," Denise protested. "In fact, I don't dance at all unless I've had a few drinks, and even then I look like Elaine from *Seinfeld*. It's bad."

"Don't worry!" Denise's friend replied. "Nobody at Zumba is going to be watching you. Nobody will give a hoot about what you look like or how good you are. We'll all be trying too hard to figure it out ourselves!"

What a great analogy for life itself. I'll say it again: Bette Davis exists primarily in your own head. She's not conspiring with your friends, family, coworkers, or random people on the street to judge you. Those people are too busy trying to survive their own crises to worry about yours!

Remember, Bette's one aim in life is to keep you limited. Bette doesn't do risk. She loves the comfort of the box, she is afraid of others' judgments, and she will do anything not to be rejected or criticized. She is a part of you, and she'll try to lure you back to the box whenever you See—and pursue—New Achievable Possibilities. Be prepared to challenge Bette so that you can create your future on your own SNAP-tastic terms.

Endnotes

1   Johnson, Erik. "Book Summary: *Thinking Fast and Slow.*" 2001. Accessed January 27, 2016. https://erikreads.files.wordpress.com/2014/04/thinking-fast-and-slow-book-summary.pdf.

2   "Lefkoe University: Learn how to eliminate beliefs for good." *The Lefkoe Institute.* Accessed February 23, 2016. http://www.lefkoeuniversity.com/.

3   Lefkoe, Morty. *Re-Create Your Life: Transforming Yourself and Your World with the Decision Maker Process®.* Kansas City: Andrews and McMeel, 1997.

"THERE MAY BE PEOPLE WHO HAVE MORE TALENT THAN YOU, BUT THERE'S NO EXCUSE FOR ANYONE TO WORK HARDER THAN YOU DO."
—DEREK JETER

CHAPTER 13

Create a Living Vision That Excites You—and Take Your Fear Along for the Ride

As I think I *may* have mentioned a few times, my uncle Bobby Murcer was an outfielder for the New York Yankees for the majority of his career. When I was a kid, we would watch Bobby play ball, and although I loved seeing him on the field, it wasn't just the baseball I enjoyed. I really, really loved seeing and hearing the national anthem being performed by a different singer each game. Even when I was knee-high to a grasshopper, I thought, *Oh my gosh, yes! I want to do that...I want to be that person singing the national anthem.* I'd picture myself walking out onto the pitcher's mound and belting out the most inspiring national anthem that Yankee Stadium had ever heard.

You know the next part of the story. For a large portion of my adult life, performing was relegated to the back burner. I had almost forgotten about my childhood dream of opening a game for the Yankees when, in 2008, Uncle Bobby passed away. Up until the very end, he'd remained with the Yankees organization as a TV announcer, and his death jarred something loose inside of me. You see, during his battle with cancer, Bobby's vision was to live long enough to announce just one game in the soon-to-be-completed new Yankee Stadium. He died in July of 2008, the day before my birthday, and 10 months before the new stadium opened.

Uncle Bobby's vision, combined with his death, reignited the vision I'd had more than 40 years ago. I couldn't get that vision out of my head, and I couldn't get my newfound excitement out of my soul.

Maybe you've noticed: When you have a vision that excites you, it excites other people too. That was certainly the case with Rick. Fast forward a bit to the 2009 World Series: The New York Yankees versus the Philadelphia Phillies. I had just turned on the TV and was ready to watch the deciding game. If the Yankees triumphed (which, by the way, they did), they'd be the 2009 World Series Champions. Then Rick yelled at me from the dining room. "DeDe! I want you to sing the national anthem for the New York Yankees tonight!"

"Huh?" I was looking at the pre-game broadcast, and I was pretty sure it was way too late for me to fly to New York and sing anything.

"DeDe, will you just come in here for a second?" Mostly to humor Rick, I walked into the dining room…and saw that he had set up a mock stadium, complete with Yankee fans. Well, they were candlesticks with Yankees hats on them, but still! How could I say no? Rick pulled out a video camera, turned it on, and said in his best announcer's voice, "Ladies and gentlemen, would you stand and direct your attention to the dining room of the Murcer Moffett household for the singing of our national anthem? Tonight's anthem will be sung by DeDe Murcer Moffett, niece of the late, great Yankee Bobby Murcer."

It may sound like a soundbite, but in a SNAP Rick's makeshift stadium turned into the real thing for me. I closed my eyes and smelled the freshly cut grass. I heard the roar of the crowd (or maybe that was background noise from the TV). I saw cutie patootie Derek Jeter and all the other fabulous Yankees and Phillies lined up with their hats over their hearts. Then I took a deep breath, swallowed my butterflies, and belted out the best possible national anthem I could muster. It was a good thing I hit all the right notes, because Rick put that video on You-Tube! He also suggested that we send a copy to my publicist, who could send it on to the New York Yankees. Wait, what?

Who's that walking toward me? Are you kidding me? It's Bette. Bette Davis is coming right toward me, and she's carrying a box. But this time, with the image of myself singing in Yankee Stadium fresh in my mind, I said with confidence and conviction, *Oh no you don't, Bette! You get the SNAP out of here right now. And don't let the door hit you on the way out.*

As you know, thanks to the incredible work of my publicist, Kelly Burleson (who also happens to have been my best friend since the day we were born), I got that call from the New York Yankees! Once we both stopped screaming and jumping up and down, I devoted myself to preparing as though my life depended on this performance. Of course I spent a SNAP-ton of hours singing, but a surprising amount of practice also took place inside my head. Remembering how "real" everything had felt that night in our dining room, I continued to visualize myself performing in Yankee Stadium every single day. This living vision was instrumental to my success.

Oh Say, Can You See DeDe Sing?

I was serious—Rick really did put my dining room performance on YouTube. You can watch it here. (Notice the candlestick "fans" behind me!) https://www.youtube.com/watch?v=w0Q-u85DF5Y

You can also watch me live my dream of singing the national anthem in Yankee Stadium here: https://www.youtube.com/watch?v=Mg0m9-nkJjY

Let me assure you: "Living" in your vision really works. It's not the same thing as staring at a bunch of inspirational pictures tacked to a board or throwing your intent out into the universe. Creating and rehearsing your vision involves concentration and commitment. While most of the effort takes place in your mind, it can tire you out and make you break a sweat. It can also take you from sorta-confident and kinda-prepared to ready-to-kick-ass-and-take-names.

That's why I've included this tactic in my book: I believe it has the power to excite you, motivate you, and prepare you to tackle your real-life challenges. Here's how to make visioning work for you.

When Are Living Visions Useful?

The short answer is, mental visioning is a great tool to help you achieve just about anything you want to do. It can help prepare you for any of the SNAP scenarios we've discussed in this book, from having a difficult conversation with your boss to giving a speech to passing a test to living on a budget. Actors, singers, and other performers use visioning to hone their crafts. CEOs use it to prepare for important meetings and presentations. It's even becoming a widespread tool to help Olympic athletes train for competition.[1]

Create a Realistic Scenario in Your Mind.

When I say realistic, I mean as life-like as humanly possible. Let's say you're preparing to meet with a client who scares the bejeezus out of you. You'd want to ask—and answer—questions like these:

To the best of your knowledge, what does the meeting space look like? Is it clean, industrial, and modern? Or does the room's decor bear the unmistakable stamp of the 1990s? What type of table or desk will you be seated at? Are there windows? If so, what can you see outside of them?

Who will be there with you? Will your client be accompanied by any underlings? Will you bring a colleague for backup? What will their roles be: silent observers or participants? Will everyone be wearing business suits or more casual attire?

What are you smelling? Has the table just been scrubbed with industrial-strength citrus cleaner? Is there a coffeepot in the corner? Does this client tend to wear too much aftershave or perfume?

What do you hear? Is your client talkative or quiet? What tone of voice does he or she normally use? Will there be background music, the click of fingers on a computer keyboard, or the scratch of a pen on a legal pad? Will other noises like the whir of a printer or the ring of a phone be audible through the walls?

How do you feel? Stressed? Nervous? Nauseated? Downright terrified? Is the air hot or cold? What's the energy like in the room? Is everyone uncomfortable? Impatient for the meeting to finish? Eager to hear what *you* have to say?

And speaking of other people listening to you…what are you saying? You're not going to wing this important meeting, are you? (Didn't think so.) So how do you greet your client? How do you open your presentation? What questions will you ask? How will you answer the questions you know you'll get in return?

Okay. I'll stop—though I could continue to help you set the scene for several more pages. If this amount of detail feels like overkill, it's not. The point is to create a vision that engages *all* of your senses and makes you feel like you're actually living the situation for which you're preparing.

Immerse Yourself in Your Living Vision Every Day.

The Yankees may have called and requested that I be at the stadium in two months, but I wasn't waiting. I went to New York City on a daily basis. (SNAP Yes! I did!) Each day I sat in my backyard swing and transported myself into Yankee Stadium. I saw that perfectly manicured green diamond and smelled the freshly painted New York Yankee emblem on the field. I felt the green springy grass under my feet. I heard the indistinct voices of the crowd, and I also heard myself deliver a powerful, in-tune, with-the-right-words national anthem as the American flag waved in the breeze overhead.

My point is, running through your vision just once or twice won't be very helpful, no matter how detailed you make it. I encourage you to "practice" for at least three to five minutes every day. Don't give me that crap…I mean excuse. I KNOW you can spare a few measly minutes. You can engage in visioning when you're in the shower or brushing your teeth. You can sit on the edge of your bed and call up your super SNAP vision before you go to sleep. You can retreat into it whenever you just can't take another second of that stupid reality TV show your spouse insists on watching!

You want to change your life in a SNAP? It takes practice. And if you practice in the right way, you will get further, faster. So make sure you can devote your entire attention to this exercise. (In other words, visioning while you're driving to work is not an option! Eyes on the road, people.) Slow your breathing down and focus your energy inward. If you're too agitated or amped-up to concentrate, stop and try again later. Eventually, you'll find that entering your vision becomes easier, and that the mental scenarios you run through become so detailed and realistic that they're almost a 3-D experience. *SNAP Yes! Now we're talking!*

Don't Forget to Take Your Fear Along for the Ride.

This is one of the most important parts of creating and practicing a living vision: Do not (I repeat, *do not*) act like you have no fear. Don't skip through that scenario without giving your worries a second glance. Take your fear with you.

When I practiced my vision, my stomach would be in knots. As I walked out onto the field, my mouth felt dry. Every time I started to sing, "Oh say, can you see," my voice and my knees would literally shake! But I stepped forward anyway, and I heard and saw myself singing the national anthem with power and confidence. You need to do the same thing. Acknowledge your stress and anxiety. Feel your pulse speed up and notice your butterflies each time you run through your vision. Then, see yourself succeeding in spite of your fear!

Why is this so important? Because when opportunity knocks, you don't want to answer the door naked. At game time, your fear might cause you to stall out if you aren't used to dealing with it. You'll think, *This isn't what I practiced and experienced in my visualizations! I must not be as prepared as I thought. I'm not ready! Is it too late to pull the plug?*

I don't think that visioning totally eradicates fear (at least, that hasn't been my experience), but it *does* make your dread and anxiety seem less overwhelming. The more you step forward, the more you will learn to use that extra adrenaline as fuel. The human mind and body are amazing, and if you practice and prepare in the right way, they will "remember" how to perform their best even when they're under tremendous pressure.

Take Action in the Real World, Too.

Just in case you're tempted to rely solely on mind games, let me make it perfectly clear that on its own, visualization isn't enough to help you create a SNAP-tastic future. You can't just dream of acing an interview with a potential employer or directing the perfect product launch party. You need to take concrete action steps to make those things happen.

While preparing to perform the national anthem, I also hired a vocal coach and trained my voice every day for a minimum of 45 minutes. I did riffs and runs, and I sang the national anthem so many times I could perform it backwards and forwards in my sleep. (And who knows…maybe I did! You'd have to ask my husband.)

All of this helped me gain the vocal flexibility and mental confidence I needed to perform in front of a tough and gigantic audience.

So, get honest with yourself. Have you done everything you can to prepare? Have you enlisted others' help and advice? Have you taken all of the necessary action steps to give your living vision legs?

So—did my living vision work for me? SNAP Yes! In many ways, June 26, 2011, was the scariest day of my life—but it was also the day I achieved a lifelong dream. It was the day I discovered my voice again. Simply put, it was a *perfect* day because I did what I never thought I could. And I got to do it with my family, friends, and—I'm certain—Uncle Bobby watching too.

Even if you're not convinced—even if you think this strategy sounds hokey or suspect that it might not work for you—I hope you'll take your best swing. Diligently practice your living vision. It will help you create the confidence and emotions that will enable you to take your dreams out of the box and knock them out of the park. Can I get a SNAP Yes?!?

Endnotes

1   Clarey, Christopher. "Olympians Use Imagery as Mental Training," *The New York Times*, February 22, 2014. Accessed February 23, 2016. http://www.nytimes.com/2014/02/23/sports/olympics/olympians-use-imagery-as-mental-training.html?_r=0.

"BECAUSE I KNEW YOU, I HAVE BEEN CHANGED FOR GOOD."
—FROM THE MUSICAL *WICKED*

CHAPTER 14

Seek Out SNAP-ers (Instead of Running from Them)

They say that opposites attract, and sometimes I'm sure that's true (especially if you happen to be living in a romantic comedy). But we typically gravitate toward people who are similar to ourselves, don't we?

If you're anything like me, you enjoy spending time with people who are into the same things you are. It feels good to talk to others who agree with your opinions, who affirm your beliefs, and who validate your choices. On the other hand, you don't exactly get excited to hang out with folks when you don't have much in common, do you? And I'll bet you actively avoid people who intimidate you, anger you, exhaust you, and generally make you feel uncomfortable.

Who's in Your "Inner Five"?

Motivational speaker Jim Rohn famously said, "You are the average of the five people you spend the most time with," and I think he was right on the money. Your attitude, outlook, energy level, sense of humor, speech patterns, likes, and dislikes all tend to reflect those of your inner circle.

Therein lies the problem for aspiring SNAP-ers: You rarely learn much from people who are like you. And in fact, spending all of your time with a crowd of committed box dwellers can severely limit your success. No matter how hard you work to break free and build your best life, they'll drag you back down, just like crabs in a bucket.

If you're serious about living outside the box, you need to seek out people who inspire you to See New Achievable Possibilities, and who insist that you get back up and continue moving forward when you fall. Will this process be easy? Almost certainly not. (But hey—I never said SNAP-ing would be discomfort-free!) You can bet that other SNAP-ers will challenge you, frustrate you, and piss you off. At some point I guarantee you'll want to tell them to leave you the hell alone.

But I hope you'll resist that urge, because these aggravating "antagonists" are actually the allies who will push you toward increasingly higher levels of achievement, fulfillment, and engagement. Whether you want to or not, they won't let you climb back into your box.

First, Seek out SNAP-ers in the Workplace.

In this chapter I'll mainly focus on seeking out other SNAP-ers in the workplace. Not because the people you spend time with in your off-hours aren't important (they are!), but because it's critically important that you "get it right" professionally if you want to "get it right" personally.

As I've pointed out before, you probably spend the majority of your waking hours at work. The attitude you develop there follows you home on weeknights and lingers on into the weekend. If you're disengaged, distracted, and challenge-averse at the office, I doubt that you magically turn into a vibrant, productive go-getter sometime during your evening commute. *Sorry; reality bites sometimes.*

A Field Guide to Identifying Workplace SNAP-ers

So, who are the SNAP-ers in your office? Your first guesses might not be correct. SNAP-ers are *not* necessarily the wunderkinds who are climbing the corporate ladder at lightning speed, or the smooth talkers who know how to play politics and work the system. If you look closely, you'll see that "faux SNAP-ers":

- Bulldoze over people, then discard them when they get where they want to be.
- Impose their will without considering the opinions and preferences of their teammates.
- Lack an awareness of how their words and actions impact others (or, they simply don't care!).
- Rationalize their mistakes or blame others instead of taking responsibility.
- Are addicted to external rewards.
- Prioritize their own interests instead of what's really important to the company's mission, vision, and growth.

- Believe that they deserve special treatment because of their accomplishments.
- Do not encourage others to do their best (they may even impede or sabotage those they see as "threats").
- Are unable or unwilling to collaborate, compromise, or share credit with others.

Employees who fit the profile painted by this list may be skilled at racking up promotions and pay raises, but chances are they're living so far inside the box it's been years or decades since they took a step that wasn't motivated by personal or financial gain. They're terrified of being seen as vulnerable, fallible, and second-best. (For these reasons, faux SNAP-ers are often at a high risk for falling prey to dishonesty and corruption.) They wouldn't recognize their passion if it SNAP-ed them on their rosy red rumps!

So who are the *authentic* SNAP-ers in your office? They're peak performers in the true sense of the word—they are congruent in their words and actions, and you can depend on them to always put forth their best efforts. They may not be loud, but their commitment and purpose can be "heard" loud and clear. They make you feel safe because they are confident in their abilities and positive about the possibilities that exist. These are the coworkers you seek out when you're really in a bind, and who you know would never throw you under the bus.

You'll be able to recognize SNAP-ers because they:

Are solution-oriented. One of the first things you'll notice about workplace SNAP-ers is that they confront roadblocks, setbacks, and failures head-on. Instead of spewing fear, negativity, and *I-don't-wannas*, they see fresh opportunities in old *and* new problems. (You won't hear a SNAP-er saying, "It can't be done," unless she has already taken every action step forward she can think of.)

What's more, SNAP-ers' solutions often demonstrate outside-the-box thinking (*of course* they do!). Where many employees might be constrained by familiar processes and procedures, a SNAP-er might see an innovative new way to remove an extraneous step, save money, improve efficiency, or plug a hole.

Aren't afraid of mistakes. SNAP-ers understand that growth rarely happens without risk, and that sometimes it's necessary to mess up in order to learn an important lesson. When SNAP-ers *do* make a mistake, they remain accountable for their actions and don't attempt to shift the blame to others. Then they examine what went wrong, why it happened, and how they can prevent the same thing from happening in the future. You won't see a SNAP-er making the same type of error twice—though if you pay attention, you might find that a lot of your team's progress can be traced back to so-called "screw-ups."

SNAP-ers take the same approach to others' errors, too. They want their teammates to feel comfortable admitting to missteps and to see them as opportunities to learn and improve. As long as the mistake wasn't the result of negligence or malice, SNAP-ers don't waste energy blaming or berating others because they recognize that constructive feedback is much more helpful.

Understand their value and limits. SNAP-ers understand their value and how it contributes to the company's mission, vision, and growth. This means that they play to their strengths and are usually in the "right" positions at work. They'll proactively volunteer for projects or assignments they know they have the skill and experience to successfully complete. (This group doesn't hide at the back of the room hoping not to be noticed!) They also recognize when they *don't* have what it takes to achieve the desired results and are willing to ask for help.

Are not afraid of hard work. You know that coworker who doesn't require a 30-minute "power-up" time at the coffeemaker each morning, who almost never stretches his breaks and lunches, and who voluntarily asks the boss what else he can be doing to help? (Yeah, the one you and your buddies probably mocked when you were still in the box.) That person is probably a SNAP-er.

SNAP-ers don't seek the easiest way or the quickest way but the *best* way. They come to work to get things done, not to be seen. And 99 percent of the time they actually *are* busy, not hiding a gossip website screen behind an "official" document when the boss walks by.

Tell the truth, even when the truth hurts. SNAP-ers voice their heartfelt opinions and concerns, even when what they have to say isn't popular. They refuse to overpromise, sugarcoat, kiss up, or lie (either by omission or commission). And while they don't seek out tough conversations simply for the sake of confronting others, they *are* willing to have a private heart-to-heart with a teammate whose attitude or actions are dragging the rest of the group down.

For instance, when you were living in the box, you may have been guilty of shushing a SNAP-er who said something like, "I'm concerned that we're not ready to deliver what the client asked for. We *could* put together a presentation based on what our team has learned so far, but it would be a shoddy, bare-bones effort. We should either ask to extend the original timeline or put in some extra hours."

Likewise, if your boss is a SNAP-er, she'll tell you exactly where your performance needs to improve (but she'll make sure you understand why the improvements are necessary, and how to go about making them). She'll always be honest with the team about the challenges you're facing and what the consequences will be if your goals aren't met. Often, boxed-in employees wish that their SNAP-tastic colleagues and leaders would be a little *less* transparent!

Are team players. SNAP-ers empower others to do their best. They're generous with their help, advice, encouragement, and constructive feedback, even when another's success means that they themselves have to stay on the bench.

Have a healthy sense of self-respect. SNAP-ers may not be driven by the need to rack up awards, accolades, and money, but that doesn't mean they're doormats either. They stand up for themselves just as fervently as they stand up for other people, and refuse to be taken advantage of. You may have overheard your fellow office SNAP-ers politely but firmly telling a pushy client no, for instance. These are also the people who are willing to endure the discomfort of negotiating a well-deserved pay raise during their annual review instead of accepting the first pronouncement of "I don't think a raise is in the cards this year."

As you're scanning the break room and conference tables for SNAP-ers, don't discount the dark horses. Even with this list of characteristics fresh on your mind, SNAP-ers might still be the people you least expect! For instance, an introverted SNAP-er might not be the most vocal person at a meeting, but when he does speak up, his ideas are always incisive and relevant. Likewise, a SNAP-er might not be the person who's constantly telling the team what to do, but the "glue" who holds everyone together by smoothing out spats and giving encouragement at just the right moment.

If you think about what you've read so far in this book, you'll see that SNAP-ing is characterized more by one's *attitude* and *actions* than by awards, accolades, and external appearances. People are most inspiring *not* when they're prominent and perfect, but when they persevere despite roadblocks, fear, pushback, and failures.

Don't See Any SNAP-ers? Your Organization May Not Be a Hospitable Habitat.

If you've taken a close look at your coworkers but can't identify any SNAP-ers, it's possible that your company culture is driving them away. True SNAP-ers will become frustrated and leave an organization if they feel that its leadership has no intent or desire to bust out of the box. If they are consistently shut down and shut up, SNAP-ers will migrate to a leading-edge company where they will be valued and heard.

So leaders, don't forget: Smart bosses surround themselves with energetic and positive people. They aren't threatened by new ideas, transparency, and fresh talent. They realize that you are only as good as the team you have around you!

SNAP into the Group.

If you're new to life outside the box, chances are you've always avoided SNAP-ers. Why? For the same reasons this group will annoy you when you do take steps in their direction: They tell you the truth and push you. They allow you to fail but expect you to get back up (or find another team). And they sure as heck don't pat you on the head and say, "Don't worry, you can keep screwing up and doing a mediocre job!" Instead, they remind you of your own unreached potential and, through their coaching and examples, encourage you to bust through limits you've told yourself are out of reach.

In other words, SNAP-ers are concerned with your growth, not your comfort. If you can get past your instinct to run from these people, your personal and professional engagement will begin to rapidly expand. Here are a few pointers to keep in mind as you SNAP into the circle:

Remember that Bette WON'T be rooting for you. As I've said, we gravitate toward groups that will confirm our deepest beliefs. If you believe you are not qualified to be in a leadership position, for example, you are not going to hang out with leaders. You will convince yourself that you have nothing of value to add to their "smart" conversation. You will worry that they're looking down at you, and you might even believe they dislike you. You will transfer your limiting beliefs from your mind into reality, even if those beliefs are absolutely incorrect.

Meanwhile, Bette will be congratulating herself on a job well done. (*I certainly saved you from embarrassing yourself on a grand scale, didn't I, dah-ling?*) If you are going to change your behavior, you must be acutely aware that your "Bette" is going to try her darnedest to convince you that SNAP-ers are threats to your happiness, comfort, and self-esteem, and that you don't want to join their ranks. (*Just stay in your box with your boxed-in friends, dah-ling! After all, they love you!*) Too bad they don't *really* want to see you succeed!

Take it slow. SNAP-ers may be open to new possibilities, but that doesn't mean they want to attract an office stalker! (And even more than non-SNAP-ers, they value authentic, meaningful relationships.) Start spending more time with your SNAP-py coworkers by making small changes in your routine. For instance:

- Step away from the "gossip group" in the break room and join a more positive conversation instead.
- Volunteer to work on a project headed by a SNAP-er.
- Email a SNAP-er and ask if you can pick his brain about a problem or project over lunch.

- Thank a SNAP-er for her thoughtful ideas and valuable contributions (even the most introverted SNAP-ers appreciate it when their hard work is noticed!).
- Tell a SNAP-er you'd like to hear more about the concept he brought up at a recent meeting.

Let them know you want their help. Once you've begun to establish a relationship with SNAP-ers, don't be shy about asking for advice, guidance, and constructive criticism. Share your goals and explain why you value their insight. Because SNAP-ers aren't driven by "superstar syndrome," they usually make great coaches and mentors and are happy to share their knowledge and expertise.

Ask the right questions. You can learn a lot from SNAP-ers simply by observing how they complete tasks and work through change, but why not dig deeper? Ask them questions like: What inspires you? Who do you consider to be a great mentor? What do you find most challenging about this line of work? How do you stay motivated and engaged when you're having a bad day or week? How do you keep your fears from shutting you down? What are your ultimate professional goals?

Prepare to see less of your former boxmates. Once you become a fixture at the SNAP-er table, expect to see less of your complacent, comfort-driven coworkers. Your old cronies won't want to be around you when they see your purpose and priorities beginning to shift. That's right: Now *you're* the one who's reminding others of how uncomfortable their boxes really are!

You might initially be tempted to become a "born-again box jumper," but remember, some people see no value in changing their limiting beliefs. They don't really want your opinion or to become any more than they are (at least not right now!). Stay in your lane, focus on your life, and keep any comments about why others "should" join you to yourself. If they're interested in SNAP-ing, they'll step forward on their own.

The Future Belongs to SNAP-ers.

When SNAP-ers find each other and begin to work together, magic happens. They're able to communicate, collaborate, and problem-solve in a way that's impossible for ego-driven box dwellers.

If you could eavesdrop on a SNAP-tastic team, you'd hear things like, *You're right. I was wrong. That idea is better. Can you explain a bit more? I'd like to understand your perspective. This meets the requirements, but I think we can do better. Can you help? Will you let me explain how you can improve next time?* You'd find a group of people committed not only to achieving benchmarks, but to developing and nurturing meaningful relationships among themselves.

In a global economy that's driven by competition, innovation, and the ability to constantly adapt, it's impossible for one person to know or do it all. Teamwork is necessary to produce and implement the best ideas in the shortest timeframe. My point is, where they haven't already, teams of SNAP-ers will soon rise to the top. Will you be on the roster?

Finally, Take Your SNAP Home.

So, what about seeking out SNAP-ers outside the office? If you're trying to drop-kick your box at work but still spend your evenings and weekends with people who don't share or support your goals, isn't that a problem? Absolutely—but it's one that tends to resolve itself.

When you begin to focus on creating your best life instead of catering to others' expectations, what I call "No Possibilities People" won't want to hang out with you. (Yes, just like at work.) They won't be ready to face the truth about your potential—and by extension, their own. They won't feel comfortable hearing you talk about your passions and goals. They won't want to extend the support you'll need as you SNAP. They won't like hearing you say no to conversations, attitudes, and commitments that keep you close to your box.

Most of those relationships will naturally fade. Let them. Remind yourself that increasingly fewer invitations to meet up for drinks or to play basketball aren't a commentary on your worth as a person. They're simply a reflection of the growth you're experiencing.

At the same time, *do* proactively find a new flock whose feathers are more similar to your own. Take a class, join a book club, volunteer for a cause that interests you, and spend more time with people you'd like to get to know better. Your new SNAP-tastic circle may be smaller, but it will be infinitely more authentic, rewarding, and supportive. And just like your SNAP-tastic coworkers, these folks will call you on your crap instead of letting you self-destruct.

Here's the thing: I'm not a believer in tossing good people to the curb. Not everyone you hang out with is going to be a Super SNAP-er, but they *do* need to be a positive influence in your life. It takes a lot of energy and commitment to jump out of the box and stay out of the box, and you can't afford to lose your focus by fighting against negative influences. Can I get a SNAP Yes?!?

"Some things I cannot change,
but 'til I try, I never know."
—From the musical *WICKED*

CHAPTER 15

When You Get Your Wake-up Call, Don't Smash Your Phone

It's zero-dark-thirty, and suddenly you're jolted awake by the worst sound in the world: your phone's alarm. You have two choices: turn off the alarm and get out of bed, or throw your phone against the wall and go back to sleep. (We've all been there. Even if you've never actually smashed your phone, I know you've wanted to.) Fortunately, one ignored alarm usually isn't that big of a deal. You oversleep, rush to get ready, and give your boss a sheepish apology for dragging into work late. No real harm done.

But at some point in your life, you'll probably encounter other kinds of wake up-calls, and ignoring them can be much, much riskier.

What Is Your Life Trying to Tell You?

As we've discussed, living in your box—or even "just" bargaining with it—is dangerous. Sometimes your box slowly sucks the life out of you through disengagement, powerlessness, and hopelessness. Other times, being boxed in causes you to engage in destructive decisions and behaviors that send you heading straight for the edge of a cliff (and a fiery crash at the bottom). Either way, when your box is calling the shots, life will send you wake-up calls saying, *This isn't the path you should be on! Wake the hell up and turn around while you still can!*

I can predict with a very high degree of certainty that you'll want to ignore life's wake-up calls. After all, change forces us toward the unfamiliar and the unknown. It's usually disruptive and difficult. Sometimes it's downright painful. And it's *always* stressful and risky. (Ummm… aren't those all of the things you were trying to avoid by living in your box in the first place? Of course they are!)

So I get it. I understand why you'd want to smash your phone, pull the covers over your head, and keep living your less-than-happy, sometimes-crappy, numbed-out life. I did just that for over 24 years. Life sent me many wake-up calls in the form of unhealthy relationships, nights I couldn't remember because I was blackout drunk, and a grinding sense of unhappiness I couldn't shake. I refused to acknowledge every single alarm…

…Until I got a wake-up call so loud that ignoring it was more painful than answering. When Rick called off our engagement because of my drinking, I knew I had gone too far. The best thing to happen to me in decades was slipping out of my reach. Was I at rock bottom? I don't know. I sometimes think we can ride our boxes all the way to our deaths. (And thank goodness, I'm still here to tell you my story.) But I *was* in enough pain to know that I didn't want to spend the rest of my life living with this particular regret. It was time to face what I had been avoiding and do the hard work of changing and rebuilding my life.

My point is, turning off your alarm will not cause any of your problems to disappear. So SNAP yourself before life snaps you!

What Does a Wake-up Call Sound Like, Anyway?

The good news is, wake-up calls usually don't start out as ear-splitting fire alarms, complete with flashing lights and sprinklers. In the beginning, they're fairly low-volume reminders. When life tells you it's time to SNAP, the first few reminders might "sound" like this:

- A performance review that was a little less positive than you'd hoped.
- Constructive criticism from a coworker or boss.
- A concerned comment from your spouse that you might be working too hard or moving in the wrong direction.
- Realizing that your first instinct is to reach for a drink, a smoke, or a pill each evening when you get home from work.
- Justifying or ignoring another person's bad behavior instead of confronting him or her.
- Lacking the energy and motivation to engage in activities you used to enjoy.
- Realizing that your kids aren't coming to you as often with their problems and successes.
- Looking at your calendar and thinking that you aren't excited about any of the events and responsibilities you see there.

It's all too easy to ignore these early warning bells. Sometimes, they just don't seem serious enough to force you out of your comfort zone. You can easily convince yourself that making a SNAP-y change probably wouldn't be worth the effort, pain, and risk.

Other times, you can see the writing on the wall but you're afraid of the possible consequences of SNAP-ing: You might have to fire someone. You might have to figure things out on your own. You might have to slow down the pace of building your career. You might have to rethink your dream. None of these are minor considerations, but here's what I know: A problem left unattended almost always gets worse. And the worse things get, the more we want to hunker down in the box with our fingers in our ears yelling, "Lalalalalalalala! Shut up, world. I can't hear you!"

Answering Early Takes Courage.

In some ways, it takes bigger balls of courage to answer life's wake-up calls when they're still at a low volume than it does to acknowledge them when they're damaging your eardrums. Early on, you have to consciously *choose* to take the more difficult path. Later, you may find that you have only one option left!

I can assure you that eventually your wake-up call *will* be so loud that you can no longer ignore it. It might "sound" like:

- A serious illness brought on by an unhealthy lifestyle.
- Crippling anxiety and/or depression resulting from a day-to-day life that makes you miserable.
- Addiction.
- A broken marriage.
- Lost friendships.

- A financial crisis.
- A derailed career.

For example, let's say you start a business with a partner. Soon, you catch this person telling little white lies about "business purchases" she has made, and when you ask why she wasn't honest, she offers little justification for her behavior. (Just in case you're wondering, that's your first low-volume reminder!)

But instead of heeding the warning, you convince yourself it's not *that* big of a deal. *So what if my partner dipped into our business account to buy clothes? She DOES need to "dress to impress" when meeting prospective clients and vendors.* Meanwhile, her spending patterns continue. And then—surprise, surprise—one day you wake up to find that your partner has embezzled all the money you put into the company. Now you're out of business, and your partner is out of the country.

Maybe you're thinking, *Well, if I were part-owner of a business, I would never allow something like that to happen.* Okay, my snappy friend, try this example on for size.

Your boss asks if you'd be willing to work on the account of a big corporate client. You prefer the more intimate, one-on-one nature of working with your company's small business clients, but you readily agree to your boss's suggestion. After all, the project in question will last only a few weeks, and you'd rather be compliant than contrary. Your boss and the client are both pleased with your work, but you're left feeling frustrated and cold after working within the corporation's bureaucratic structure. (That feeling of dissatisfaction is the first low-volume wake-up call that you're not moving in a SNAP-tastic direction.)

Over the next few years, you agree to work with several more large clients because you want to be a "team player," and because you're reluctant to make waves. Gradually, almost without realizing it, you become your company's "corporate client expert." You can't remember the last time you worked with a small business—or the last time you didn't dread going to work. Your health has also declined because you rely on sugary snacks to boost your energy, and after a long grueling day at the office the last thing you want to do is go to the gym. As you're rushed to the hospital after suffering a heart attack, you think, *How did my life get this far off track? Why didn't I take charge and move in a different direction when I still had the chance?*

Wake-up Calls DO Work.

The longer you wait to answer a wake-up call, the more likely it is to turn your life upside down. That's a fact. But I don't want you to finish this chapter thinking that wake-up calls are all doom and gloom. Even when they're ear-splitting, they can and often do spark SNAP-tastic change. As you know, my own wake-up call led directly to my (finally!) breaking up with Mr. Cabernet Sauvignon. It also helped me build the career I enjoy today. Here are a few more real-life examples of painful wake-up calls that led to positive change:

- At one of my recent speeches, I met a woman who told me that she'd always wanted to get her psychology degree but kept putting it off for various reasons. Those reasons were some of the usual suspects: She wanted to wait until she was more financially stable to contemplate a career change. She didn't have time to go back to school. She didn't want to disrupt the rhythm of her family life while her kids were in elementary school. And so on and so forth.

  Finally, at 55 this woman was diagnosed with breast cancer. She was forced to confront the fact that she might not have much more time to accomplish her dream. This was the wake-up call that finally prompted her to SNAP and get her butt in school. Today she is cancer-free, has that degree, and is helping others via art therapy.

- One of my friends, Karen, chose to sacrifice a lot of her dreams in order to support her husband. Their family moved with his job, taking her away from education and career opportunities. She shouldered the lion's share of childcare and housework to accommodate his long hours and late nights. And then she was blindsided with divorce papers.

This wake-up call forced Karen to acknowledge that she had been living her life based on the limiting belief that she couldn't make it on her own without her husband's income. She knew that she finally had to step up and take control of her livelihood, finances, and more. She found the courage to obtain paralegal training, and now she is self-sufficient, more confident, and happy.

Wake Up and Smell the Tobacco.

By the 1970s the health risks of tobacco use were already well known, and Big Tobacco needed celebrities to help push their products. Seduced by cars, fancy dinners, and—of course—big money, my uncle Bobby Murcer agreed to be a spokesman for Skoal smokeless tobacco. Skoal really poured on the limelight. Bobby starred in commercials and even cut a record called "Skoal Dippin' Man." (It was a real hit in New York—for two weeks it was the most requested song on the city's country-western radio station!) Bobby walked his talk, too—for 10 years he was a big Skoal user, even though he was aware of tobacco's dangers.

Then in 1978, Bobby had part of his lip cut out because his doctors thought he might have cancer. Fortunately the problem was caused by a stopped-up saliva gland, but this was still a wake-up call for Bobby. Over the next few years, he quit kidding himself about tobacco, he quit using, and he quit pushing products for Skoal.

Bobby also took his wake-up call a step (or should that be a SNAP) further: He used it to benefit as many other people as possible by convincing lawmakers in our home state of Oklahoma to beef up the regulation of tobacco sales to minors. In 1997, the Oklahoma State Senate passed the Bobby Murcer Tobacco Addiction Prevention Bill. And in March of 2006, Bobby's influence helped ban smoking in most public restaurants in Oklahoma City.[1]

The Next Time It Rings, Answer Your Darn Phone.

Wake-up calls are going to happen for the rest of your life. (Yes, even if you've been trying to live outside the box for years—Seeing New Achievable Possibilities does not magically protect you from making choices that take you in the wrong direction!) Wake-up calls also happen for a reason. So pay attention. Be on the alert for a soft "ring, ring, ring!" that might be easy to ignore amidst the chaos of daily life. And when you hear it, have the big balls of courage to answer with a SNAP Yes! Who knows how much time, money, energy, and heartache you might save yourself and others in the future?

Endnotes

1   Murcer, Bobby. *Yankee for Life: My 40-Year Journey in Pinstripes.* New York: HarperCollins, 2008. 232-38.

"GRIEF NEVER ENDS. BUT IT CHANGES. IT'S A PASSAGE, NOT A PLACE TO STAY. GRIEF IS NOT A SIGN OF WEAKNESS, NOR A LACK OF FAITH. IT IS THE PRICE OF LOVE."
—ANONYMOUS

CHAPTER 16

Yes, It's Possible to Keep Seeing New Achievable Possibilities After Experiencing Pain and Loss

I want to warn you upfront: There's some tough subject matter ahead. In this chapter, we're going to talk about pain, loss, and grief. Why? It's inevitable that sooner or later, your world will be shaken to its core by something HUGE like the death of a loved one, a major injury or illness, divorce, betrayal, addiction, or abuse. (That's assuming you haven't experienced one or more of these things already.)

Wake-up Call or Not, Pain Can Stop You in Your Tracks.

In the last chapter, I wrote that some of life's loudest wake-up calls can come in the form of disease, divorce, addiction, etc. I definitely believe that if you have the mental, emotional, and physical resources to keep moving forward after something like this happens to you, it's important to "answer your phone." But I *do* want to acknowledge that sometimes the impact of a wake-up call can be so great that it temporarily stops you in your tracks. In this chapter, we'll talk about how to deal with your pain so that when you're ready, you can acknowledge that alarm.

I also want to point out that sometimes devastating things happen through no fault of your own. A heart attack might result from genetic predisposition—not from an unhealthy lifestyle. A partner might blindside you with divorce papers and the admission that he or she has been engaged in an affair for years.

When these kinds of crippling, all-consuming events happen, they can punch your SNAP-tastic intentions right in the gut, leaving you gasping for breath and wondering what in the hell happened to the future you had planned for yourself. Your ability to move forward will be temporarily frozen. You'll probably want to run screaming back to your box. *And that's okay.* Needing to feel as safe as possible is a *normal* reaction. But what about later? What about after the socially prescribed "grieving time" is over? What then?

Now, I am going to assume that none of this speculation is new to you. You've probably done your share of fretting about the inevitable. For example, when you hit middle age, you can't help but think about Time's relentless march and how it's also impacting loved ones who are ahead of you on the journey. When you allow yourself to think about it at all, you grapple with uneasy thoughts like, *I love my mother so much and I know she can't have* too many *years left. How will I go on? Will I be able to function at work? Who will love me unconditionally now?*

If you're a parent, the thought has almost certainly crossed your mind (however fervently you wish you could squelch it) that your child could die. *Would I even want to go on living—much less engage joyfully in life? In fact, would I ever feel joy again? I might as well quit my job because it wouldn't matter anymore. Nothing would.*

And of course death of a family member isn't the only form of loss. Far from it. Our pets die. Our marriage crumbles. Our health slowly (almost imperceptibly) disintegrates. Our youthful beauty fades. Our kids grow up and move away. And yet, among all these losses, we are expected to keep moving forward. And guess what? WE CAN. We don't have to stop living, learning, engaging, growing, and improving when hard times hit. What's more, we shouldn't.

I'm not saying it's easy to get back into a fully engaged life when you've been sucker-punched by loss—but as many wise people have pointed out, nothing worth doing ever is. (And yes, you and your life *are* worth it.) Even in the best of times, stepping out of your comfort zone is tough, right? Add a big old smothering blanket of grief and it can feel like an hourly (even a minute-ly, if that's a word) struggle. But I have seen people face terrible losses, collapse to the ground (metaphorically and literally) in deep mourning, and get back up to courageously take on life once again.

I don't mean some sort of half-assed half-life. I mean living, loving, and working to their fullest ability. In turn, they've been able to help many others through their stories. I'd like to share a few of those with you now.

You Have to Engage Your Feelings to Move Through Grief.

My friend Mary Chippich is an event planner for Aesynt (an au-tomation-in-healthcare company). In 1997, Mary lost her young son. During the following months and years, Mary saw many individuals in her grief support program dive deeply into their boxes. Rather than face and feel the overwhelming pain of losing a loved one, they lived in the past, buried themselves in denial, and engaged in a variety of numb-ing-out methods. According to Mary, they were stuck in their grief and unable to move forward.

I know you'll gain a valuable measure of wisdom from reading Mary's story. Here's what she wants you to know, in her own words. Many of the tactics she used to work through her grief and pain can help you deal with the loss of any loved one.

"On December 24, 1997, I lost my one-year-old son, Will. That day an unwanted guest moved into my house and has refused to leave. His name is Grief. It's been a long road with more downs at times than ups, but somewhere along this journey, I found my 'new normal' and learned how to live without my son.

"When Will first passed away, many people told me it would get better. *Yeah, right*, I thought. In those early days of grieving, you can't imagine ever *not* feeling that raw sting of fresh loss. Now, I'd say that 'better' is probably not the right word to use because it doesn't get bet-ter…you just learn to live with your loss.

"People ask, 'How did you get over your loss?' I have to chuckle inside, because the death of a child (or any loved one) is something you never get over. The 'easy' starts to come when you find your new normal and learn how to live with this raw hand life has dealt you. Actually, saying that it gets 'easy' isn't accurate either; it's more that the sting of those early days will slowly fade in intensity. But the pain never goes away entirely—and you don't want it to. To not grieve would be to not love. I wouldn't trade my time with Will for anything.

"Here are some of the things that have helped me face and feel my pain, and move forward in spite of it:

1. **Decide to move forward.** I decided early on that I did not want to spend the rest of my life feeling the way I did. Life had to get better. Having that mindset helped me find ways to move forward through my grief. I had days where I felt I was moving backwards, and I knew that was okay because that's how grief works. But after a day or two sliding backwards, I'd pick myself up and move forward again.

2. **Know that pain doesn't look the same for everyone.** I had to come to the realization that not everyone grieves the same way, at the same pace, or even in the same order of 'phases' (Shock/Denial, Pain/Guilt, Anger/Bargaining, Depression/Loneliness, etc). This is important to remember when you are grieving with someone else. Will's father didn't grieve the same way I did. You must move through each stage, but the order doesn't matter as long as no one is destructive to themselves or others.

3. **Write about it.** I wrote to Will every day for months. Grief brings out your ugly, 'shameful' feelings and thoughts. I would write down exactly how I was feeling and what I was thinking. I didn't hold anything back. It was my way of unloading and getting it out. Over time, I began writing less and less frequently.

   One thing I learned in talking to others who were grieving was that I was not the first person to have 'horrible, shameful' thoughts and feelings. And I am sure I will not be the last. Really, there is nothing to be ashamed of…you're hurt and devastated. Let it out.

4. **Visit the grave.** I did this because Will is my son, and it made me face Will's absence. I still had the feeling that I needed to take care of him. Visiting his grave helped me feel like I was still doing my job as his mom. I was making sure he was okay. The grass was trimmed, flowers were planted, and weeds were pulled. Over time, this need faded and that is okay, too. That is moving forward.

5. **Find a method to move through grief.** Many people find comfort in joining a grief support group, or participating in one-on-one therapy. I tried four support groups and didn't feel like I fit. So I grabbed my Bible and every Max Lucado book I could find and dug in. I talked to my pastor when I needed to. That worked for me—it may or may not work for you. You have to find a method that is comfortable and right, and only you can decide what that is.

6. **Learn not to take others' reactions *too* personally.** People will say dumb things with the best of intentions. Your friends and family will want to do and say something that will make you feel better. What they fail to realize is NOTHING will make you feel better. Some people will not speak of your loss fearing they will make you cry. Others will want to remember with you. Whether you talk or not, you *will* cry, and your friends and family need to know this.

7. **Tell people what you need/want.** If you want to talk about your loved one, tell other people that it's okay to talk about them. If you don't want to talk about your loss, tell people that, too. My biggest fear was that Will would be forgotten. The more he was talked about, the better I felt…even when I cried.

8. **Face it and feel it.** I think this is the most important lesson I learned. In order to move forward, you have to face your pain and really FEEL however it is you are feeling. There will be times when the pain is unbearable. There will be noises that come out of you that scare you. These noises come from the depths of your soul. If you've suffered a great loss, you'll understand what I'm talking about. This is part of the grieving process. You have to feel your loss at a primal depth in order to move forward.

This happened to me while I was sitting in my car at Will's gravesite. Being in the car, I could scream as loudly as I wanted and pound on the steering wheel as hard as I wanted. When it was over, I felt a thousand pounds lighter and I slept better that night than I had since before Will passed. It was then that I figured out that feeling my pain was key. From that day on, if I felt sad, I allowed myself to feel sad. If I felt happy, I allowed myself to laugh. I knew Will loved me and wanted me to be happy. I did not have to feel guilty when I had a good day.

"Grief is all about choices, and YOU are in control even when you feel like you are not. Grief is not easy. It hurts and it's scary at times. But you can survive it. You can move forward and find your new normal. Your loved one will always be with you. You will always love them. You will always miss them. But you *can* live a happy, joy-filled life again. Keep moving forward.

"'You either get bitter or you get better. It's that simple. You either take what has been dealt to you and allow it to make you a better person, or you allow it to tear you down. The choice does not belong to fate; it belongs to you.'" —Josh Shipp

How can you apply Mary's lessons to your own life? Which of her strategies and tactics might help you come to terms with a loss you have experienced? Do you have any new insights on the importance of "feeling your feelings" instead of squelching them?

Bobby Murcer: Playing Through Pain Can Help You Stay in the Game.

It was 1979, and the Yankees were playing against the Baltimore Orioles. But this wasn't an ordinary game. Earlier that day, the Yankees had flown to Canton, Ohio, to bury their catcher and team captain Thurman Munson. He had been killed in a tragic airplane accident, and the whole team was in shock after his unexpected loss.

After the funeral, manager Billy Martin pulled my uncle Bobby Murcer aside and suggested that he sit that night's game out. Billy knew that Bobby was one of Thurman's closest friends, had spoken at his funeral, and had been awake for several days straight—so it was a thoughtful offer. (And because of everything my uncle had been through, maybe Billy didn't believe Bobby had it in him to effectively contribute to the team.) But to Billy's surprise, Uncle Bobby refused to stay on the bench. While he was certainly exhausted, he felt a strong need to play the game for Thurman.

Despite their best efforts, the game didn't begin well for the emotionally drained Yankees. By the time Bobby stepped up to the plate in the bottom of the seventh inning, his team was in serious danger of losing.

Can you imagine the pressure Bobby was under with two outs, two men on base, and two strikes against him? (Can you imagine how easy it would have been to sit the game out in the first place?) But he stayed focused and determined, and when he got HIS pitch, he stepped forward and made solid contact. The ball went back...back...way back...

yes, it was a three-run homer! Bobby had just brought his team to within one run of the Orioles.

At this point, Bobby could have rested in the fact that he had done his job and contributed in a big way. He could have let thoughts like, *What do they expect? I'm worn out, I'm heartbroken, and I'm tired* dominate his mind. He could have sat down and let someone else step up to the plate. But he had a vision for what he wanted to accomplish, and that vision was fueled by a love for his friend Thurman. So he stayed in the game despite his pain.

Talk about a nail-biter. In the bottom of the ninth, still down a run, the Yankees once again had two men on base. (Believe it or not, the same two men who had been on base during the seventh inning.) Who do you think steps up to the plate? Uncle Bobby. Again, Bobby patiently waited for his pitch. When it came, he smacked the ball down the third baseline all the way to the fence. Both runners scored, winning the game for the Yankees. The crowd went wild! (For good reason, this is still one of the games that is played over and over on the YES Network as a Yankee Classic.)

Here's the thing: Despite his heroic performance, Bobby was in great pain that night. But he took his pain and used it. He allowed it to push him forward instead of sideline him. I'm certain that he played to win that night not because it was his job, but because of his love for his friend and teammate Thurman Munson.

I am also certain that afterward, Bobby grieved and (as Mary Chippich stressed) engaged all of the painful emotions that accompany the loss of a dear friend. But through his willingness to channel his pain toward a goal, he helped those on his team, those in the stands, and the entire Yankee Nation to grieve, honor, and remember Thurman Munson in the most special of ways.

Here are a few important things I've learned about pain from my uncle Bobby:

- Pain allows you to feel your true capacity for love. The valleys of grief highlight just how high the peaks of cherished relationships really are.
- Sometimes shutting down is not the best way to process pain. Grief often needs to be actively balanced by something positive. Work—when it's meaningful work—can give you the purpose and focus you need to keep functioning after loss, and to keep hopelessness and helplessness at bay.
- Confronting the people, places, and situations that remind you of your grief isn't always painful—it can also be therapeutic.
- Pain can move you in a direction that not only heals you, but allows you to change and heal the lives of others, too. By reminding you of life's briefness, pain can motivate you not to squander the time you have left.
- Grief *doesn't* mean that nothing in your life can be good again. In fact, it's likely that the person you lost would be proud of the positive things you are able to accomplish.

Jo Khalifa: When Life Gives You Lyme, Make Coffee.

Jo Khalifa is the founder and CEO of Mojo Roast Coffee (www. mojoroast.com), a Westhope, North Dakota-based business that creates customized roasts for customers. Jo has been building her business for 14 years and has succeeded in establishing herself as a major player in the market. Recently, she was named a Woman of Distinction by the YWCA. (Oh, and did I mention? She's also a mom of seven.)

In 1996, Jo was diagnosed with Lyme disease—seemingly out of the blue. In Jo's words, Lyme disease is like "MS, Alzheimer's, and fibromyalgia all descending on you at one time." Jo was assailed by extreme joint pain and chronic fatigue. For months on end, she couldn't get out of bed or work a full day. Her physical struggles were compounded by the frustration of not being able to find medical answers for her pain, and by the fact that no cure was in sight.

Given the abrupt loss of her health, Jo certainly had a great excuse to stay in bed, give up, and become a victim of her disease. But she didn't. You see, Jo has a deep belief that everyone is a gift to someone else in the world. As long as you are alive and breathing, you can serve as an example and a blessing to others.

And boy, does she ever. In spite of the many challenges Lyme disease has thrown in Jo's path, philanthropy and community are huge parts of her life. Mojo Roast and Jo herself serve as resources for cancer organizations, the military community, the homeless, the hungry, domestic abuse victims, community daycares, and more.

"Waking up in agonizing pain and pushing through the day hasn't been easy," Jo admits. "But although my body is beaten up and not working properly, I still have a brain and spirit that can advise and steer my business. I also have the ability to laugh at myself. (I haven't figured out how I have gotten through each day, and for some reason that hits my funny bone!)

"I don't have time to dwell on negative aspects of life because there's so much to be done to move myself and others forward," she continues. "That's what life is about. I've taught my kids this too—how to be a go-giver. I want to lead by example, because a lot of people depend on me. There are so many people who have it worse than me, and I won't be my own Grim Reaper. I know that no matter what day it is, someone needs me. If I quit, I might cause someone else to quit, too. And then there would be one less person that someone in great need would have to rely on."

There are three important things I hope you'll take away from Jo's story:

- **Living a fulfilled, passionate life does not mean that you ignore your pain.** Jo deals with the debilitating physical symptoms of Lyme disease every day, and she openly acknowledges what she's struggling with. If she were to think and act as though nothing had changed since her diagnosis, I suspect she'd quickly become demoralized and disengaged. No one has the energy to maintain such a significant illusion for long!

  When you're honest about your pain (whether it's physical, mental, or emotional), you've taken the first important step toward *not* letting it drive you back into your box. In order to See New Achievable Possibilities, you have to accept reality as it is, not as you'd like it to be.

- **Positive energy is a powerful force.** Jo is one of the most relentlessly positive people I know. She wakes up every day and sees fresh opportunities to make herself and her world better. That's powerful medicine! Our thoughts and attitudes *do* influence our physical health through the hormones and chemicals our bodies produce, as well as through their impact on our immune systems.

  Whether you're dealing with a physical ailment or not, be sure to proactively care for yourself by choosing to focus on what brings you happiness, hope, humor, gratitude, and purpose. All of those things can make you feel better in a SNAP!

- **Getting "outside" yourself can be very therapeutic.** To some extent, you have to be selfish when dealing with pain of any sort. If you don't acknowledge and meet your emotional, mental, and physical needs, you'll burn out. But once those needs *are* met, it doesn't do you any good to spend the rest of your time wallowing. (That just leads to stay-in-the-box emotions like bitterness, helplessness, hopelessness, and jealousy.)

As Jo demonstrates, being active and altruistic is a great way to keep your focus on new possibilities. Helping others will enable you to maintain balance and perspective in the midst of tough times—and it's also a valuable tool to help you boost your mood and health. Believe it or not, philanthropy can lead to benefits including a longer lifespan, increased happiness, better pain management, and lower blood pressure![1]

What NOT to Do When Dealing with Grief

Before ending this chapter, I also want to share some of my own advice, in the form of what *not* to do when your SNAP-tastic plans are derailed by grief, loss, or pain.

Over the course of my life, I have dealt with my share of heartache and loss. I lost my father to lung cancer when I was 26 and he was 47. I've also lost my grandfather, grandmother, two uncles, and a lifelong friend to cancer. In my youth I had a relationship with a jealous, controlling partner who was emotionally, verbally, and physically abusive. I've experienced divorce. I lived through decades of alcohol addiction, and I am still affected by the sometimes-daily struggle of ongoing recovery.

Having spent many years dealing with my own pain in unhealthy ways, I hope I can help you avoid some of the same pitfalls I've fallen prey to.

Don't downplay your pain. (*Yes, I pointed this out after introducing you to Jo Khalifa, but it definitely bears repeating!*) Have you ever noticed that we humans have a tendency to downplay the extent of our heartache and pain? It certainly happens when we're at work. Wouldn't you go to great lengths to avoid crying at your desk or admitting during a meeting that you're *not* doing okay? To a lesser extent this also holds true in our relationships with friends and family members. How often have you answered the question "How are you?" with a faux-cheerful "Fine!" even though you were anything but? Even to ourselves, we frequently try to deny just how deeply we've been affected.

Look, I get the fact that nobody wants to be around a "Debbie Downer." I understand how uncomfortable it can be to admit to yourself and others that you're having trouble coping with the curveball life has thrown your way. But take it from me: *That strategy doesn't work.* Denial isn't effective *at all.* (Not to mention, it's the partner of all addictions!)

I'm not saying you need to send out a company-wide memo that your father's death has knocked you to your knees, or that you should hang a sign on your front door letting visitors know that you're likely to be in a fetal position because of your recent divorce. I *am* saying that you should talk privately with your boss about taking a few vacation days if you need them. I *am* saying that you should let your supportive group of friends and family know when you're struggling, and how you'd like them to help. (You'd be there in a heartbeat if your friend needed a shoulder to cry on, right? I thought so!) And I'm *definitely* saying that when pain and grief invade, you have to see these unwanted visitors as necessary and important in order to move past them. If you don't, you'll be numbing down and living in a box for the rest of your life.

Don't beat yourself up if you need to press "pause." Under normal circumstances, I'd say that there is no such thing as standing still when you're trying to SNAP. Either you're moving forward toward new possibilities, or you're edging back toward your box. Dealing with large amounts of pain and loss is the exception to that rule.

When you need mental or physical healing, you might want to press the pause button on your goals. They will still be there when you are ready to work toward them again. (In fact, forcing yourself to keep accomplishing action steps can be a form of denial that causes long-term burnout and affects your physical and mental health.) Right now, your priority is safeguarding your well-being.

Don't force yourself to abide by someone else's version of "handling it." As Mary Chippich pointed out earlier in this chapter, everyone handles pain and grieves differently. Keep that in mind when you receive advice—well intended or otherwise—to help you "keep living" and "feel good" about life.

No matter what circumstances you're dealing with, there is no deadline by which you should be "over it." Likewise, as long as you aren't engaging in harmful or destructive behaviors, there is no "right" way to grieve or process your emotions. It's okay to be loud, to cry, to punch a pillow, or to slip on your jogging shoes and run until you're exhausted! It's okay to take a break from your everyday life and go on vacation. It's even okay to continue taking small action steps toward your goals if you know that you feel more alive when you keep your mind and body occupied.

Don't hold yourself to your previous vision. After you experience a major loss or painful life circumstance, your values and priorities may change. You might find that your old SNAP-tastic goals just don't seem that important anymore, and that you feel a strong desire to move in a different direction. Remember Betsy Jourdan, whose story I shared in Chapter 11? Losing both her father and an important father figure prompted her to rethink her career path and pursue a newfound calling in the funeral services industry. I know other people whose pain has sparked a SNAP moment that drastically changed their work/life balances, their exercise and eating habits, and the way they engage with other people.

My point is, it's okay to SNAP in a new direction. You aren't betraying your old goals or your pre-loss self. Thank them for the experience and motivation they provided you, and gracefully let them go.

I wish I could just SNAP my fingers and make all of your struggles, pain, and losses go away. I wish I had all the answers and could offer you formulas and techniques that would help you to instantly heal. But I don't. All I have are my experiences and the experiences of the people to whom I have introduced you on these pages.

I have faith that these words will lighten your load and help heal your heart. My hope is that you won't feel so alone in this big old world, and that you will realize we are all here struggling together—and doing our best to keep stepping forward and Seeing New Achievable Possibilities in life. Can I get a SNAP Yes?!?

Endnotes

1   Goldman, Leslie. "4 Amazing Health Benefits of Helping Others." *HuffPost OWN*, December 28, 2013. Accessed March 01, 2016. http://www.huffingtonpost.com/2013/12/28/ health-benefits-of-helping-others_n_4427697.html.

CONCLUSION:

SNAP for the Long Haul

Sometimes people ask me what the most difficult part of living outside the box is. As you know from reading this book, there are a lot of possibilities to choose from: facing and overcoming a lifetime's worth of regret, saying "hell no!" to staying in your comfort zone, telling Bette Davis to bite you and to zip it, uncovering your passion and figuring out how to weave it into your daily life, taking uncomfortable risks…I could go on and on.

But no, none of these things—tough though they may be—top my list. **Without a doubt, the most difficult part of living outside the box is *staying* outside the box over the long haul.**

Once you realize how much your boxed-in life sucks, it's easy to get fired up about Seeing New Achievable Possibilities. You can't wait to ditch your disengagement and limiting beliefs! You're excited to find your spotlight and stand in it! Your initial momentum might be strong enough to carry you through several weeks or months of action steps and disruptive choices.

But then you slowly begin to lose steam. Studying for your recertification is exhausting—you'd rather just lose yourself in mindless television shows each evening. Living on a stricter budget is getting really old, really fast. You miss the relative ease and anonymity of doing only the bare minimum at work. Dealing with the judgment of others is harder than you thought. And who wants to regularly leave the gym feeling like they've been run over by a truck? *3-2-1…Cue the box bargaining!*

After you've drop-kicked your box, how do you stay away from it for the rest of your life? How can you keep your energy up and your focus sharp in spite of life's fender benders, sucker punches, and quagmires? How can you possibly sustain your SNAP for a whole year…or five years…or twenty…or more? This is an impossible task, right? *Come on, DeDe. Get real.*

No, it's not impossible—although I get why you might think that. I thought the same thing when I stopped drinking back in 2007. How in the world would I sustain my enthusiasm and not choose to drink again…ever?

Well (ironically!), I found my answer in the words of Dos Equis' Most Interesting Man in the World: "Stay thirsty, my friend." You've got to stay thirsty for ways to expand your talent and your abilities. You've got to stay thirsty for more knowledge and experiences. You've got to stay thirsty for more love and more joy and more fulfilling relationships.

To help you stay thirsty, here are some powerful strategies to help you sustain your SNAP power over the long haul:

Keep putting fuel into your SNAP tank. Vehicles need gas to keep running. Bodies need nourishment to keep functioning. And your SNAP-tastic attitude needs regular refreshment to stay vibrant. In other words, assuming this book has inspired you, you can't just put it back on the shelf and expect your new and improved attitude to last forever. Make sure you're consistently exposing yourself to ideas that motivate, educate, and fulfill you.

First of all, keep seeking out reading material that makes you think and challenges you to change. (I've included a list of my recommendations below.) Open this book and re-read a chapter when you need a pick-me-up. Watch videos. Attend conferences and webinars. Subscribe to free newsletters. (If you'd like to receive mine, you can sign up on my website, www.dedemurcermoffett.com.) And keep in mind that SNAP fuel doesn't have to be "motivational" in nature. It can also pertain to a specific goal you're pursuing. For instance, an article in a professional journal or the autobiography of a groundbreaker in your industry might put enough pep in your step to get you over the next hump.

SNAP into a Good Book.

Here's a short list of books I've found to be inspiring, thought-provoking, and educational over the course of my own SNAP journey. The next time you're looking for good reading material, I encourage you to pick one of them up!

- *The Energy Bus: 10 Rules to Fuel Your Life, Work, and Team with Positive Energy* by Jon Gordon
- *True North: Discover Your Authentic Leadership* by Bill George
- *A Cup of Cappuccino For the Entrepreneur's Spirit: Volume 1: Find Your Passion and Live the Dream* by Jeretta Horn Nord

- *Leading From the Edge: Global Executives Share Strategies for Success* by Annmarie Neal
- *Choices and Illusions: How Did I Get Where I Am, and How Do I Get Where I Want to Be?* by Eldon Taylor
- *Essentialism: The Disciplined Pursuit of Less* by Greg McKeown
- *The Barefoot Spirit: How Hardship, Hustle, and Heart Built America's #1 Wine Brand* by Michael Houlihan and Bonnie Harvey
- *Stairway to Success: The Complete Blueprint for Personal and Professional Achievement* by Nido R. Qubein
- *Secrets of Your Family Tree: Healing for Adult Children of Dysfunctional Families* by Earl R. Henslin, William Henry Cloud, John S. Townsend, Dave Carder, and Alice Brawand
- *Fearproof Your Life: How to Thrive in a World Addicted to Fear* by Joseph Bailey
- *Yankee for Life: My 40-Year Journey in Pinstripes* by Bobby Murcer
- *When the Yankees Were on the Fritz: Revisiting the "Horace Clarke Era"* by Fritz Peterson

Avoid updates from the box. Just as it's important to keep exposing yourself to things that help you learn and grow, it's also crucial to *avoid* things that bring you down. I'm not saying that you need to go on a media blackout or turn around and walk the other way when a known

Debbie Downer approaches you. I'm just urging you to (as your mom might have said) make good choices over and over again.

If the evening news is bringing out your inner pessimist, turn it off. If scrolling through your social media feeds makes you fear for the future of humanity, put down your smartphone. If a conversation is veering into "I can't" territory, don't buy into it. If the topic of discussion at the water cooler is about how no one can ever get ahead, chuckle to yourself and walk away. "Little" choices like this can have a surprisingly big impact on your desire to crawl back into the box or keep SNAP-ing.

Stay plugged into the SNAP-er circle. No matter how long you've been out of the box, this will never *not* be a big deal. If you move to a new town or are transferred to a new department, for instance, immediately start the search for bold, out-of-the-box colleagues and friends. Don't make the mistake of thinking that you have enough momentum or experience to go it alone. (SNAP-flash: You don't!)

No matter how much you've already accomplished, you *need* people in your life who are aware of your goals, who will encourage you to reach them, and who will call you on your crapola when you begin to box bargain. Without fellow SNAP-ers in your corner, you'll always be fighting an uphill battle.

Pace yourself. SNAP-ing is a lifelong marathon, not a short-term sprint. You're much more susceptible to the lure of the box when you're tired and spread thin. Here are a few tips to help you stay energized:

- Listen to your mind and body, and ease off the gas if you know you need some R&R. (If it helps, you have my permission to go to bed early or book that massage!)
- When you're mapping out your long-term strategy, be sure to build in an off-season—such as a week or two with no client meetings. (Also, hello, vacation!)

- Realize that you don't have to say yes to every opportunity. A thoughtful "no" or "not right now" will be one of the most valuable items in your SNAP-ing toolkit.
- Resist the urge to compare yourself to other people who are on similar paths. The fact that a coworker seems to be making more upward progress than you does *not* necessarily mean that you need to push yourself harder or that you are going the wrong way. We all have our own unique paths to walk and our own challenges to overcome.
- Don't try to do it all at once. As long as you aren't facing set-in-stone deadlines, set your sights on one or two goals at a time. *This month I'm going to focus on speaking up more at work. This month I'm going to focus on establishing a sustainable fitness routine. This month I'm going to focus on volunteering at the animal shelter.* Etc.

Keep your SNAP on the sunny side. SNAP-ing is supposed to make your life better and more fulfilling. (In other words, taking action steps toward your goals shouldn't become just another dreaded to-do list.) So as often as possible, I urge you to:

- Celebrate your successes and reward yourself for achieving milestones—no matter how big or small.
- Partner with people who make you feel good about who you are and where you're going.
- Find the humor when you trip and fall. If you're going to look back at a situation and laugh at it later, you might as well laugh now, too.
- Remember that not all achievable possibilities have to be serious or related to a major life change. Allow yourself to pursue "fun" goals too, like taking a ballroom dance class with your partner or joining an improv comedy group.

Take good care of yourself. Often, people will spend weeks or months designing a comprehensive action strategy. They'll map out each step forward and account for almost every possible contingency. But they fail to consider the one thing that can derail their plans faster than saying "the box wants you back": their own physical fitness.

I'm not saying that you have to be in marathon-running shape or that every meal you eat needs to be certified organic with no additives. I *am* saying that if you're sick and tired, your ability to do great things will be severely compromised. Not only will you reach your physical breaking point sooner; your mental health and motivation will also suffer. (Just think about how much more difficult it is to summon a smile—much less extra energy—when you have a cold!)

It doesn't matter how inspiring your goals are if they aren't *achievable*. (The "A" in SNAP is there for a reason!) So as you actively design your best life, make sure that it includes reasonable and sustainable amounts of exercise, a (mostly) healthy diet, and enough sleep.

Personally, I'm a huge sweet freak and I love cottage cheese. But in order to keep my mind sharp and avoid the downward spiral that sugar causes, I often choose to forego that chocolate bar. (Though I do indulge every now and then—as should you!) I also crave dairy on a regular basis, but since it causes all types of drainage problems, I typically avoid it. As a speaker and singer, that's a frustration I don't need. And hey, I loved drinking too! But just because you like the way something tastes or makes you feel, that doesn't mean it will help you reach your long-term goals.

No matter what people say, you can't always have your cake and eat it too. Yep, I know it sucks—but so does being too sick and tired to do that thing you will regret *not* doing later!

Stay flexible. As I've mentioned before, your goals will probably grow and change as *you* grow and change. This is especially true as you learn and accomplish new things over the course of the coming years and decades. Do you want the same things now that you did in your teens or twenties, for instance? Didn't think so. Consider this a gentle reminder to pause every now and then and ask yourself if you're still heading in the direction you want to go. If you find that you're moving forward primarily out of habit or obligation—not excitement—it's probably time to change course.

When in doubt, I find it helpful to think about my life backwards. What do I want to be known for when I die? What do I want to remember? What legacy do I want to leave? Will I like the person I have become? When seen in this light, it's usually clearer which fork in the road I should take.

Focus on the future, not the past. The past is where all of your regrets live, and in hindsight, those regrets tend to stick out like bright red sore thumbs. Dwelling on them is a surefire way to sap your motivation and energy. The real kicker is, every hour you spend beating yourself up over past mistakes and missed opportunities is an hour you haven't spent moving toward your goals. When you catch yourself taking mental trips back to your boxed-in days, consciously shift your focus back to the SNAP-tastic future you're working to build. Close your eyes, tap into your *why*, and allow those strong emotions to flood you with fresh motivation.

(That said, there are a couple of good reasons to review your past: reminding yourself of how far you've come and harvesting valuable lessons from past mistakes so that you don't make them again!)

Ultimately, remember that everyone struggles to stay motivated to keep pushing forward. (Yes, even people who seem to get everything they want just by snapping their fingers.) If you find yourself tempted to dive back into your box on a regular basis, let me assure you that there isn't a gene or essential skill you're missing. The only thing that separates those who do from those who don't is a daily choice to keep moving further away from the box.

So wake up each day and decide to keep Seeing New Achievable Possibilities wherever you go. It's time to let go of your past and grab hold of your future. It's time to start loving your life and, more importantly, yourself. Now is the time to find your spotlight and stand in it. Can I get a far-from-final, incredibly bodacious, super-loud SNAP Yes?!?

Acknowledgments

Behind every great event, talk, accomplishment, and book are a whole host of people who have tirelessly helped make your vision and dream SNAP into reality. That's certainly been the case for me. Without the insight, expertise, support, and pushback of many people, this book would not have been possible.

First and foremost, I thank my husband for his continued support of my recovery and my career. You keep me striving to stay out of the box and encourage me to be more and more of my authentic self. Thank you for loving me.

To my mom, thank you for the hundreds of conversations that have helped me see what's really important in life. You've always reminded me that success does not lie in how many talks I give, books I write, or songs I sing. Success is leaving people feeling better when I walk away. Your love and support are what sustain me.

To my unbelievable group of SNAP-y girlfriends, Kelly, Robbi, LeaAnne, Jo, Stella, Jeretta, and Bonnie, I would not be where I am today without your love, support, honesty, and friendship. When I am with you, I believe I can fly!

To my two nieces, Jessie and Kristen Murcer: You two girls are the epitome of SNAP-ers! You are authentic, heart-centered, hard-driving athletes and students. When I'm up against a tough decision, I often stop and say, "What would my nieces do?" Then I step forward and take my shot. I love you both, as Mema would say, "To the moon and back."

To my brother: No one makes me laugh more than you. And honestly, are you really that funny? SNAP Yes! you are!

Thank you to all the contributors who courageously told your stories throughout this book. For many of you, it was a painful journey back in time, but you were committed to sharing your experiences so that others might be comforted as they travel along this crazy path we call life. I sincerely appreciate you all!

To my uncle Bobby, whom I miss dearly, thank you for having the courage to follow your lifelong dream. I wish you knew what an impact you made on the lives of others. When people talk about you to me, they don't talk about your baseball stats; they talk about how kind and courteous you were to them. They remember how you took time to talk or sign an autograph when other players wouldn't. They tell me what a class-act you were and how you made them proud to be Yankees fans. I'm so proud to be your niece.

To Dottie DeHart, Meghan Waters, Anna Campbell, Ashley Lamb, and the entire team at DeHart & Company Public Relations: Wow, what a journey! I don't know a more talented group of people. Thank you for all of your hard work on bringing this book into being, from helping me fine-tune my messaging and strategy to structuring, editing, and proofreading each chapter. You made me dig deeper than I thought I could. You made me laugh harder than sometimes I should have. You took my thoughts, my SNAP processes, and all my stories and organized them in a way that is easy to digest and fun to read. I can't wait to work with you on my next book!

To my readers: Thank you for going on this SNAP-tastic journey with me. My hope is that you will find relief from your anxiety, fear, and stress; that you will become confident in your talent and abilities; and that you will finally find the courage to jump out of that damn box and into your own spotlight of success. Can I get a SNAP Yes?!?

About the Author

DeDe Murcer Moffett began her career as a corporate sales executive. For 25 years she sold millions of dollars of products, services, and financial portfolios for companies including Toyota Material Handling, Waste Management, State National Insurance Company, and Auto Financial Group. But for 24 of those years, DeDe hid her lack of passion and purpose by developing a three-bottle-a-night alcohol addiction. After hitting rock bottom, DeDe decided to say

SNAP Yes! to the hard work of overcoming her alcoholism and transforming her life. She has since found the sweet spot where passion, prosperity, and happiness meet.

Today, DeDe enjoys a successful career as an international speaker, author, and entrepreneur. Using her own experiences as a platform, she specializes in giving others the tools to embrace disruptive and long-lasting change. DeDe's powerful, provocative content and dynamic, high-energy style help individuals and businesses identify barriers to success, overcome obstacles, and increase engagement.

DeDe is also a trained performer and has sung the national anthem for many professional sports organizations, including the New York Yankees. (This opportunity is offered only to a very select group of singers; past invitees include Kristin Chenoweth, James Taylor, and Billy Joel.) Additionally, she has shared the stage with many celebrities, entertainers, and thought leaders. Her album, *I Believe*, and first book, *Wisdom Wedgies & Life's Little Zingers*, are available on Amazon. DeDe is currently collaborating with award-winning composer and lyricist Daniel Maté to develop a one-woman show, *If I Stop Then Who Am I?*

DeDe and her husband, Rick, live near Denver, CO, with their four-legged kiddos: Sheba the cat and Asta the German Shepherd. They are committed to improving the health and lives of dogs (and their owners!) through their customized, all-raw, non-processed, farm-to-bowl Raw Dog Food and Company business (www.rawdogfoodandco.com).

To learn more, visit www.dedemurcermoffett.com.

Book DeDe to Speak

Voted "Meeting Planners' Favorite Speaker"
by *Meetings and Conventions* Magazine

DeDe Murcer Moffett is a change expert specializing in employee engagement and professional success. Through keynotes, workshops, and master classes, she helps individuals and businesses remove internal and external obstacles and transform old problems into new possibilities. She is known for her out-of-the-box presentation skills, which incorporate music and audience participation to demonstrate that getting outside your comfort zone is not only crucial for success; it's invigorating for life!

Why is DeDe such a crowd favorite? Because people are tired of typical and predictable lectures. They want an experience they can be a part of. When DeDe gets entire audiences out of their boxes (and seats!) and up onto the stage, their engagement, fun, and energy levels go from 0 to 60 in a SNAP!

DeDe is known as a powerful voice in the speaking industry because she understands on a personal level the problems, challenges, and stresses that employees face. Like 83 percent of today's workforce, she was disengaged in her career for 25 years (and an alcoholic for 24 of them). When audiences hear DeDe's story, they can directly relate to her experience of being overwhelmed and to her desire to "numb out" from it all. Many nod their heads in agreement and say, "Yes, that's me!"

Let DeDe help your employees ignite their SNAP potential and give them the tools to sustain that momentum for the long haul. She can tailor her message to fit the needs of your audience and/or field. To see a listing of DeDe's speech offerings, visit www.dedemurcermoffett.com.

Wisdom Wedgies & Life's Little Zingers

Daily Motivation That Gets Stuck in All the Right Places!

Are you struggling to find joy and passion in your personal or professional life? Do you ever have one of those days when you need a little boost of courage to keep stepping forward? If so, *Wisdom Wedgies* is exactly what you need. This funny but thought-provoking book is perfect for the office or home (and it makes a great gift, too!). Each page is filled with powerful bite-sized messages that will help you move past fear, doubt, and confusion so that you can live a fuller and more fulfilling life. Face it: When all the news is negative, you simply can't afford to miss a daily dose of inspiration!

Here's what readers are saying about *Wisdom Wedgies & Life's Little Zingers*:

"This is a very humorous, delightful read while still being extremely insightful and introspective."
—Sunny Anne

"The author is so honest about her addiction and life struggles and has turned that around into something positive, light hearted, and inspirational…This book is for everyone…A fabulous read!"
—Jo Khalifa

"Humorous, touching, and inspirational…these little zingers really make you think…I laughed and cried all the way through it."
—Barbara Green

Order your copy today from Amazon.

Made in the USA
Middletown, DE
24 July 2017